D1576946

AROUND THE WORLD IN 80 DAYS

•

A RACE THROUGH THE GREATEST RUNNING STORIES

Damian Hall is an author and outdoor journalist who contributes regularly to *Outdoor Fitness* and most of the running, fitness and outdoor press. The midlife-crisis ultramarathon runner is happiest running long distances in lumpy places and has completed the Spine Race, the Dragon's Back Race and UTMB. But his children only seem to remember the time he got beaten by a 13-year-old at parkrun.
www.damianhall.info

Daniel Seex has been a professional illustrator for over three years and has worked for a number of high-profile clients including Google, Channel 4, Johnnie Walker and Chivas Regal and for cycling publications *The Ride Journal* and *Boneshaker*. Daniel works primarily in pen and ink, adding colour and texture digitally and often building a picture from multiple drawings. He lives in Edinburgh with his partner Julia.
www.thejoyofseex.co.uk

AROUND THE WORLD IN 80 DAYS

A RACE THROUGH THE GREATEST RUNNING STORIES

Written by Damian Hall

Illustrated by Daniel Seex

Aurum
Press

Quarto is the authority on a wide range of topics.
Quarto educates, entertains and enriches the lives of
our readers— enthusiasts and lovers of hands-on living.
www.QuartoKnows.com

First published in Great Britain
2017 by Aurum Press Ltd
74–77 White Lion Street
Islington
London N1 9PF
www.quartoknows.com

A catalogue record for this book is available from the British Library.

ISBN 978 1 78131 674 0

10 9 8 7 6 5 4 3 2 1
2021 2020 2019 2018 2017

Interior design by: Neal Cobourne
Printed in China

For Indy and Leif

CONTENTS

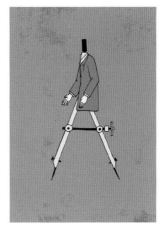

1

The Hakone Ekiden
(2 January since 1920)

On this date in Japan, people with usually no interest in running switch on the television and settle down with their New Year *mochi* (rice cakes) to watch the Hakone Ekiden. The TV audience share is similar to the Super Bowl in the US and brings the country to a standstill with spectators lining the length of the course.

It's both Japan's biggest annual sporting event and one of the toughest mass-participation endurance events in the world. The Hakone Ekiden is a 135-mile (217km) relay race shared between university teams (male only) of 10 runners. Run over two days, it starts in the centre of Tokyo, travelling to the foot of Mount Fuji and back.

Although the Hakone dates from 1920, *ekidens* really took off in Japan as part of the post-World War II rebuilding process, with companies setting up sports teams in an effort to help raise worker morale. To help runners train, relay races – ekidens – were arranged, modelled on the courier system of Japan's Edo period (1603–1868) that saw runners relay messages between Kyoto and Tokyo.

Today *ekidens* have surpassed the marathons in popularity in Japan, with the Hakone Ekiden being the runners' – and the viewers' – favourite.

2

The American Deer runs 11 miles in an hour
(6 January 1845)

William Howitt, also known as William Jackson and more commonly referred to as 'The American Deer', became the first man to run 11 miles (18km) in an hour – and live to tell the tale. A runner named Bettridge had previously achieved the feat – but died very shortly afterwards, from 'over-exertion'. This American Deer was actually born in Norwich, England, but the Brit adopted his moniker after a short trip to the US.

The 11-mile race took place on the Hatfield turnpike road near Barnet, England, with William Sheppard, 'the Birmingham pet', also running. Marshals were placed a mile apart, holding a handkerchief which the runners touched before turning around, and spectators lined the course. Sheppard was ahead for most of it, but stopped at 10 miles (16km), having clocked a new world record of 53:35 (minutes:seconds). It's unclear whether he stopped due to exhaustion or because he'd miscounted the miles and thought the race was over.

3

Ricardo Abad, the Spanish Forrest Gump
(8 January 1971)

Born on this date, Spain's Ricardo Abad claims the world record for most marathons run on consecutive days – a not-to-be-sniffed-at 607. His project started in October 2010 as '500 marathons in 500 days and he ran at least one marathon in each of the 50 Spanish provinces, breaking the previous record of 366 set by the Belgian Stefaan Engels (before that it was Abad's record, with 150). He ran his 500th on 12 February 2012, but then decided to carry on, aiming to reach 1,000. He had to abandon his quest at 607, however, after failing to secure sufficient funding for the project.

Abad's achievement is even greater than it initially sounds as his 607 marathons were fitted around eight-hour shifts in a factory, which could be morning, afternoon or evening, so he sometimes ended up running two marathons in under 12 hours.

Abad has twice been nominated for Prince of Asturias Awards, annual prizes awarded for notable achievements in the sciences, humanities and public affairs.

4

The Spine Race
(11 January 2014)

The Spine Race is a foot race along England's 268-mile (431km) Pennine Way National Trail, which traces the Pennines, the country's 'backbone'. It claims to be 'Britain's most brutal race', and competitors are allowed up to seven days to complete it. Northern England may

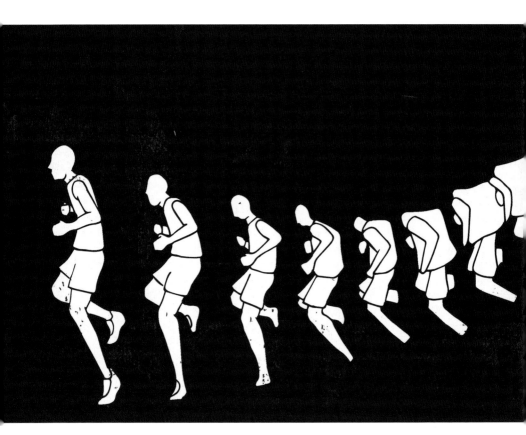

not be Arctic wilderness, but the event is continuous (meaning the clock is always ticking) and the race is known for extreme weather, the real threat of hypothermia (from the country's often underestimated wet cold) and the wild hallucinations of sleep-deprived runners. Exhausted competitors have been found by Mountain Rescue on remote hilltops in their sleeping bags, while others have run into the back ends of cows. The 2014 race was won by sleep-allergic Czech adventure racer Pavel Paloncý in 110 hours and 45 minutes, and he successfully defended his title the following year.

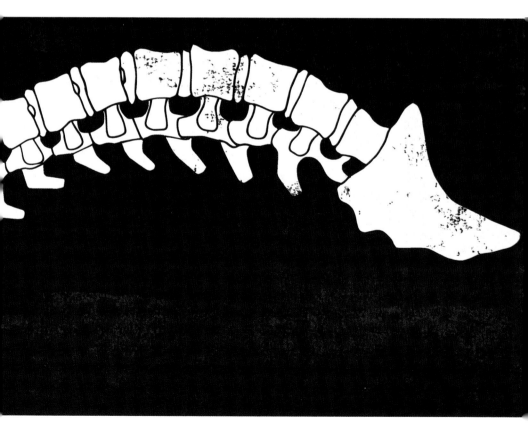

5

Charlotte Teske runs a world record time
(16 January 1982)

On this date, Germany's Charlotte Teske ran a world record (according to the Association of Road Racing Statisticians) of 2:29:01 (hours: minutes:seconds) to win the Miami Marathon. The joint biggest moment of her career happened the same year at the Boston Marathon when, finishing the race in what she assumed was second place, behind hot favourite Grete Waitz (see page 70), Teske was surprised when officials placed a laurel wreath over her head and ushered her to the winner's stage. Waitz had dropped out ahead of Teske, leaving the spoils to the German. 'I feel very sorry,' she said afterwards. 'I didn't beat her really.'

Paediatric nurse Teske represented West Germany at the 1984 Olympics as well as European and World Championships, but would never repeat the success she achieved at road running on the track. She would win city marathons in Frankfurt, Hamburg (twice each), Berlin and Munich. Her preparation included running over 137 miles (220km) a week, plus strength training and aerobics. After her running career she retrained as a physiotherapist.

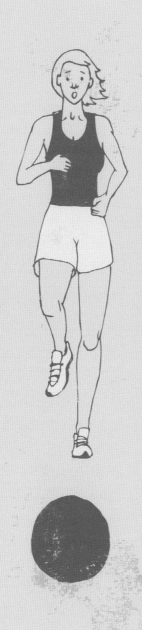

6

Super Swede Dan Waern
(17 January 1933)

Born on this date, Swedish middle-distance runner Dan Waern became the first Swede to run a sub-four-minute mile, recording 3:58.5 in 1957 – albeit three years after Briton Roger Bannister broke the famous barrier. For his efforts, Waern was awarded the *Svenska Dagbladet* Gold Medal – an annual award 'for the most significant Swedish sports achievement of the year'.

The former amateur boxer also ran the 1,500m at both the 1956 and 1960 Olympics, placing fourth in the latter. In 1958 he won 1,500m silver at the European Championships and broke a three-year-old world record in the 1,000m with 2:18.1. He would do better the following year with 2:17.8 – another world record.

His appearances guaranteed crowds in Sweden and he accepted payment to run at a one-off gala. This was against the strict International Association of Athletics Federation amateur rules, however, and he was disqualified in 1961, retiring to work on a farm and do fitness coaching for a local football team.

7

The legendary Deerfoot dies
(18 January 1897)

Native American Indians were great runners, doing so to hunt, fight and carry messages. But much of their greatness isn't known to us because it wasn't done on circular tracks or recorded in notebooks. That is except for Louis Bennett, also known as Deerfoot and, according to Edward Sears's book *Running Through the Ages*, 'the greatest American distance runner of the nineteenth century'.

Deerfoot's most noted achievements took place in England on a 20-month tour in 1861 and 1862, where he was pitted against the best long-distance runners of the time, in what became the Deerfoot Running Circus. He defeated nearly all of them. Though many races were fixed in his favour to increase his aura and market the events, the American was no imposter. He set world records for 10 miles/16km (51:26), 12 miles/19km (1:02:02) and one hour (11 miles, 970 yards/18.6km) – the latter record lasting 34 years.

The Native American would appear in a wolf-skin cloak, eagle-feather headdress, bell-festooned red apron, necklace and earrings, and parade around a venue. He ran in moccasins rather than the spikes popular at the time and would release signature 'war-whoops'.

Deerfoot was known for his 'spurting' technique during races – essentially dashing ahead, then waiting for others to catch up, then spurting off again.

The American was a sure-fire crowd-puller and his fame attracted high society to the sport of pedestrianism, with the future Kind Edward VII inviting him for dinner. The extraordinary American eventually died, aged 69, on this date.

8

Christopher Chataway, star of 1954, dies
(19 January 2014)

The British runner, who later became a TV broadcast journalist, businessman and politician, only had a brief career, but one full of significant moments. He was one of Roger Bannister's two pacers when the four-minute mile was broken, won gold over 3 miles at the Commonwealth Games and set a 5,000m world record of 13:51.6, in so doing beating the legendary Vladimir Kuts by 0.1 seconds – all in

1954. And all apparently on four training sessions a week and despite being a smoker. He had such an impact in this year that he became the first winner of the BBC's Sports Personality of the Year award.

In 2006, at the age of 75, he ran the Great North Run half marathon in 1:38:50 – still faster than most people decades his junior. Chataway passed away in 2014.

The Great Trans-Canada Race
(1 February 1921)

A crowd of 2,000 turned out in Halifax, on Canada's east coast, to cheer off husband and wife Jenny and Frank Dill, the final entrants of the Great Trans-Canada Race. They were two of only five contestants – the other three already well ahead – in the 3,645-mile (5,866km) pan-Canadian race to Vancouver.

A welcome distraction from post-war hurt and high unemployment, the extraordinary event caught the public imagination, with regular newspaper coverage and large crowds turning out en route, offering sustenance, new shoes and even lifts – though apparently none were taken – to the contestants, comprising a postman and his son, Jack and Clifford Behan, and athlete Charles Burkman.

Jack and Clifford thought they'd won, 138 days of hiking later, when they arrived on the west coast. Three days later, however, the Dills arrived, in four days less overall.

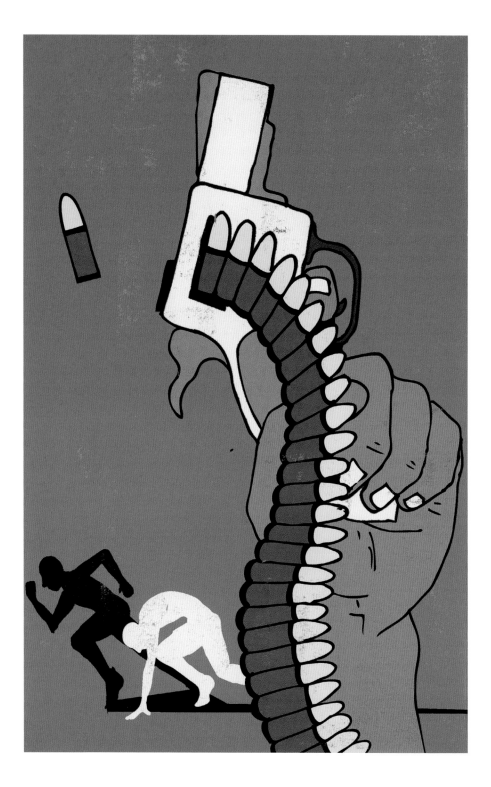

10

Thirty-two false starts
(4 February 1851)

Bellevue, Manchester, hosted a memorable 150-yard (137m) contest between sprinter William Hayes, known as 'the Ruddington Hero', and Charles Westhall, the first man to break 4:30 for the mile on a track.

It was a cold day and the track was covered in snow, which may have accounted for many if not all of the 32 false starts. After an hour of surreal non-running, the runners finally left the line in a manner satisfying to the officials. Only for Westhall to promptly slip over. Hayes had a lead of 3 yards (2.7m) at the half-way mark.

In a moment you imagine Hayes rather regrets, he turned to his pursuer and put his hand on his nose in a mocking gesture. Westhall wasn't in a mood to be ridiculed and, fired up, responded by catching and passing his rival.

After winning, Westhall was said to press his hand on his 'nether end' in a gesture of retaliation. He had also recorded the fastest time for 150 yards: 15 seconds flat.

11

'Iron' Joss Naylor is born
(10 February 1936)

'The hardest man in the hardest sport' is how many see Joss Naylor and the British sport of fell running. Naylor, who would earn the nicknames 'King of the Fells', 'Iron Man' and 'Iron Joss', grew up under the shadow of England's highest fell (i.e. mountain), Scafell Pike.

Yet his youth never hinted he would be a sporting legend. He was hindered by a serious back condition and rarely took part in school sports, leaving at 15 to work on a farm. He was deemed unfit for national service and at 18 had an operation to remove the cartilage from his right knee. That didn't go well: it prevented him fully extending his knee and gave him an unusual running gait. And yet he knew – and ran – the fells like no one else.

Aside from the Bob Graham Round, the most coveted fell-running record is the number of Lake District peaks scaled inside 24 hours. In July 1975, Naylor ran through a heatwave to raise his own record by nine to 72 peaks, an achievement that earned him an MBE.

Among his other records are reaching all 214 of the summits listed in Alfred Wainwright's Lake District guides in seven days, one hour and 25 minutes – in 1986 at the age of 50. And he didn't stop there. At the age of 60 he ran 60 Lakeland fell tops in 36 hours. In 2006, aged 70, he ran 70 Lakeland fell tops, covering more than 50 miles (80km) and ascending more than 25,000 feet (7,620m), in under 21 hours.

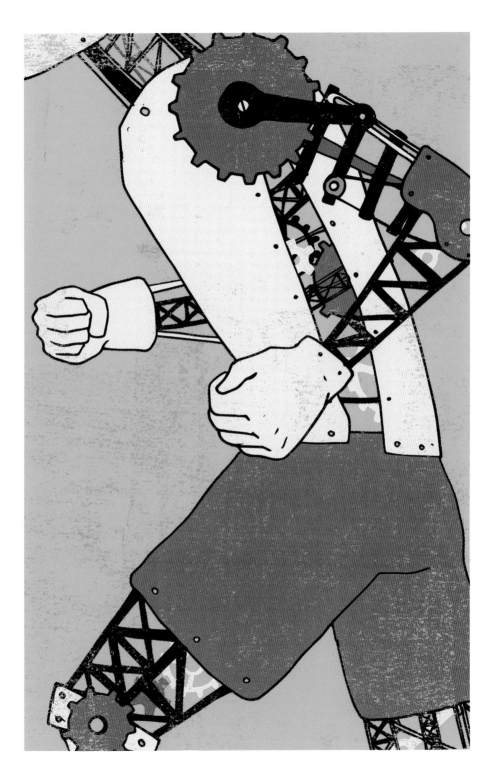

12

Yiannis 'Running God' Kouros is born
(13 February 1956)

If running has ever had a Superman, it is Yiannis Kouros. Creator of 160 world records, Kouros is the greatest ultramarathon runner of all time, if not simply the greatest runner.

Greek-born, he immigrated to Australia and rose to prominence when he won the first Spartathlon (153 miles/246km) in 1984 and the 544-mile (875km) Sydney to Melbourne Ultramarathon a year later. He's won Spartathlon four times and the four fastest recorded times for the race are all his.

Kouros has set world records from 100 to 1,000 miles (10 days, 10:30:36, if you were wondering) and every road and track record from 12 hours to six days – he still holds the vast majority of them.

He takes three months off running each year, sometimes five, and aside from events rarely runs more than seven or eight miles at a time. Impressively, he also has a talent for the arts, with a master's degree in literature, and has had many poems published. Fittingly, the Greek played the role of Pheidippides in the 1995 film *A Hero's Journey*, about the history of the marathon.

13

Cathy Freeman is born
(16 February 1973)

At the 2000 Olympics in Sydney, Cathy Freeman created not just one of the great Olympic moments, but a great moment for post-colonialism. Most of Freeman's relatives were Aborigines, her grandmother part of the 'stolen generation' forcibly removed from their families as children and raised by white parents.

As in most post-colonial countries, relations between Indigenous and non-Indigenous Australians haven't always been harmonious, but they were able to come together in 2000 to celebrate the brilliance of Freeman.

The 400m runner was the first Indigenous Australian to become a Commonwealth gold medallist, in 1990, aged just 16, and she competed in the 1992 and 1996 Olympics, taking silver at the latter. She was World Champion in 1997 and 1999, and prior to the 2000 Games had won 37 of her previous 38 finals. The expectation was huge.

There were 112,000 people inside the stadium and half of Australia watching on television. Wearing a curious hooded bodysuit, Freeman started cautiously. She seemed to tire slightly in the final 200m (219 yards) and was level with two others entering the home straight. But her strides grew in length as she powered away, the will of the host nation pushing her along, to win by nearly half a second.

The lack of smile at the finish line perhaps gave away the release of pressure, rather than pure elation, she must have felt. Overwhelmed, Freeman sank to the track and sat for two full minutes as the crowd cheered. She carried both the Australian and Aboriginal flags on a lap of honour – despite the fact that 'unofficial' flags are banned at the Games. On her upper right arm, the side closest to spectators on an athletics track, she has 'Cos I'm Free' tattooed.

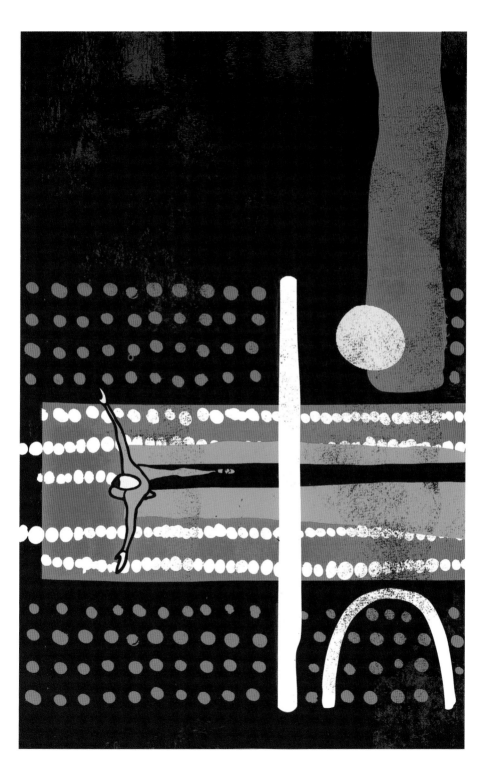

14

4,000-mile run across the Sahara
(20 February 2006)

Charlie Engle (US), Ray Zahab (Canada) and Kevin Lin (Taiwan) reached the Red Sea and the end of an incredible 4,300-mile (nearly 7,000km) run across the Sahara. Their journey, starting from the coast of Senegal, had lasted 111 days – the equivalent of two marathons a day for 100 days – and had taken them through six countries (also Mauritania, Mali, Niger, Libya and Egypt). They were the first contemporary runners known to have crossed the famous desert, and a Matt Damon-narrated documentary, *Running the Sahara* (2007), tracked their progress.

Lin and Zahab were competitive ultramarathon runners (even if the latter used to smoke a pack of cigarettes a day), but Engle had a more unlikely past. The American is an ex-drug addict, alcoholic and convict, who enjoyed running marathons but entered his first ultramarathon by accident, thinking he was entering a 10K event. And won it.

15

Pam Reed, Badwater winner, is born
(27 February 1961)

In 2002 the US's Pam Reed became the first woman to win the notoriously hot, 135-mile (217km) Badwater Ultramarathon outright – aged 41 and by a margin of five hours, setting a women's course record by nearly two hours. She then went on to win it overall again the next year, beating Dean Karnazes (see page 134) into second place.

In 2005, Reed ran 300 miles (483km) without sleep. She is the female American record holder in six-day marathons, after completing 490 miles (789km) at 2009's Self-Transcendence Six-Day Race in New York.

With five sons and her own race to direct, Reed sneaks in short training runs between school drop-offs and collections, several times a day.

16

The start of the Bunion Derby
(4 March 1928)

Billed as 'the greatest test of human endurance in history', 1928's Great Transcontinental Footrace measured 3,423 miles (5,508km) from Los Angeles to New York City in 84 daily stages of between 30 and 75 miles (48 and 120km). A $25,000 prize lured 199 runners to the start line of the 'Bunion Derby' and an unprecedented 15 million Americans would turn out to see the race.

British-born Arthur Newton was the star attraction, along with Willie Kolehmainen, older brother of Olympic hero Hannes (see page 105). Kolehmainen was out by day three, however, thanks to an absurdly fast start. Newton, too, crashed out injured with a nine-hour lead, though the star continued as 'technical advisor'.

As the event started losing money, race director Charles C. Pyles began lengthening the stages, up to 75 miles (120km) at a time, to try to complete it sooner. After 84 days, 55 runners finished, many in rags and some shoeless. The victor, Andy Payne, paid off the mortgage on his father's farm with the winnings, then retired from running after a doctor judged the race had taken 10 years off his life.

17

Edit Bérces runs on a treadmill for 24 hours
(9 March 2004)

In 2000, Hungarian Edit Bérces won the World and European 100K Championships. In 2001 she won the IAU 24-Hour World Championship. In 2002, she won the European 24-Hour Championship and (just two weeks later) set a 24-hour world record on the track and a 100-mile world record en route. Having seemingly run out of road and track races to win, in 2004 Bérces turned to the treadmill.

The Hungarian set a 24-hour world treadmill record of 247.2km (153.6 miles), which at the time was better than the men's record. She again set a 100-mile world record in the process. 'I felt like a caged bird,' she said at the time, 'who will be freed only after 24 hours.'

Although she had four breaks 'for hygienic reasons', she never once stepped off the treadmill.

18

Yohann Diniz sets a world record
(12 March 2011)

French racewalker Yohann Diniz has three European golds and one World Championship silver to his name, all over the 50km distance. He's had setbacks though. He failed to finish in the 2008 Olympics on an extremely hot day. He was disqualified at the 2011 World Championships for collecting three red warning cards, and again at the 2012 Olympics, after finishing eighth, for taking a bottle of water outside the official zone.

He probably feels he had the last laugh, as he currently holds the world records for 50km on both track (3:35:27 in 2011) and road (3:32:33 in 2014) – the latter despite stopping to ask for a Portuguese flag, in homage to his late grandmother.

19

The first (second, third and fourth) sub-2:30 marathon(s)

(21 March 1935)

There's a popular phrase in Britain that goes, 'You wait ages for a bus to come along, then three turn up at once.' So too, it seems, with running world records.

According to the Association of Road Running Statisticians, Japan's Son Kitei ran the marathon in 2:26:14 in Tokyo, hacking over four minutes off Harry Payne's world record, which had stood for six years.

Kitei's compatriot Fusashige Suzuki also broke the old barrier, with 2:27:49.

Admittedly there's some confusion over the exact dates – though they were both recorded in March 1935 in Tokyo – and whether the times occurred in the same race. But what is clear is that just a few days later, on 3 April, compatriot Yasuo Ikenaka also broke the 2:30 barrier, with 2:26:44, also in Tokyo.

Kitei would better his record in November, running 2:26:42, a time that wouldn't be beaten for 12 years.

Kitei, however, was actually Korean, not Japanese, but Korea was then part of the Japanese Empire. In 1988, under his real name of Sohn Kee-chung, he carried the Olympic torch into the stadium at the opening of the Seoul Games.

20

The first women's six-day race
(26 March 1879)

The pedestrian movement wasn't just for men. The first major women's six-day race was held on 26 March 1879 at New York's Madison Square Garden. The winner, Bertha Von Berg, received $1,000 for covering a distance of 372 miles (600km).

Only five of the 18 participants would finish, and the women were described as: 'a queer lot, tall and short, heavy and slim, young and middle-aged, some pretty and a few almost ugly'. The misogyny didn't stop there, with *The New York Times* calling the event 'cruel' and the women 'unfortunate', plus the mostly male crowd heckling unkindly at times.

Some female peds were certainly ill-prepared, racing in dancing slippers that quickly filled with sawdust. But they were also required to wear heavy velvet dresses, which undoubtedly hindered them.

The second major female six-day race became a duel between 17-year-old Amy Howard from Brooklyn and a Madame Tobias. The former was crowned Champion Pedestrian of the World in 1880 and her record of 409 miles (658km) stood for 102 years.

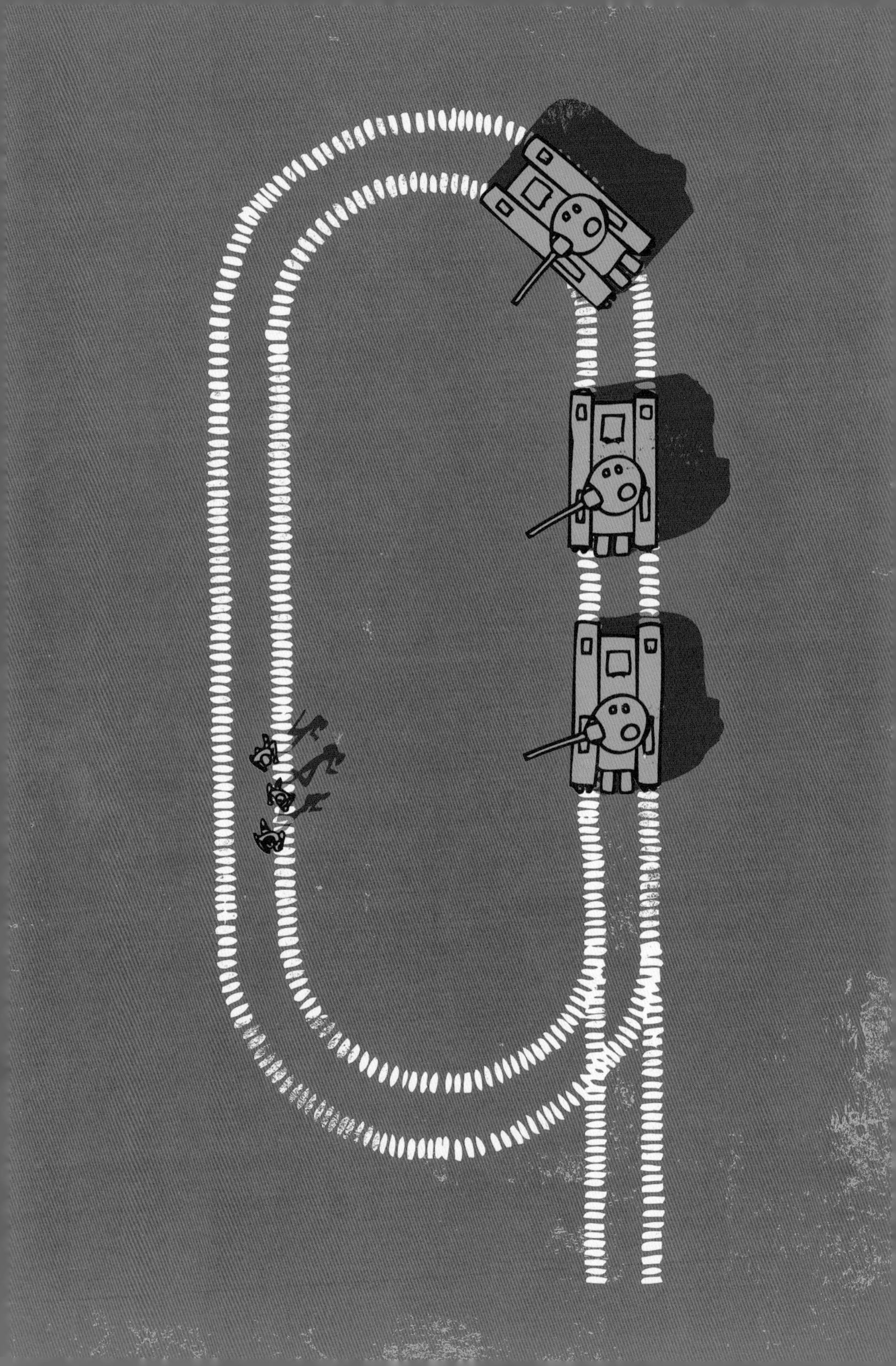

21

István Rózsavölgyi is born
(30 March 1929)

A former footballer, István Rózsavölgyi was one of the trio of Hungarian middle-distance runners – the others being Sandor Iharos and László Tábori – who broke world records in the 1950s, all coached by pioneering Mihály Iglói.

Rózsavölgyi's greatest year was 1955, when he bagged world records for 1,000m (2:19.0) and 2,000m (with 5:02.2). A year later he broke the 1,500m world record, with 3:40.5 in Tata, as well as surpassing the 3,000m world record (but being narrowly beaten to the tape).

The following year was something of a disappointment. The speedy Hungarian went to the 1956 Olympics in Melbourne as a favourite for 1,500m gold. At home, however, the Hungarian Revolution had just been quashed by the Soviet Union, which must have been a major distraction, and Rózsavölgyi failed to make the final.

Past his peak at the 1960 Olympics, he did however snare a bronze medal.

22

The fastest run around the world
(9 April 2015)

Today Kevin Carr became the fastest man to run around the world. The 34-year-old British runner set off from Haytor, Devon, in the southwest of England, in July 2013, running approximately a marathon a day for 621 days to complete his world record – and beating the previous record by just 24 hours.

Carr wore through 16 pairs of shoes, pushing all his kit along in a stroller, as he ran through 26 countries and covered 16,299 miles (26,231km). 'I have encountered some pretty scary things,' he said, 'from packs of wild dogs in Romania to the most extreme weather conditions imaginable. Most frightening of all, however, was coming face to face with bears. One of the bears stalked and then actively came for me. I had severe heatstroke in India and have twice been hit by cars.'

23

Plennie Wingo starts walking backwards
(15 April 1931)

Plennie Wingo, 31, began to walk backwards from Fort Worth, Texas, on this day and didn't stop for over a year. 'With the whole world going backwards,' he wrote in his book, *Around the World Backwards*, 'maybe the only way to see it was to turn around.'

Wingo said the hardships of the Great Depression motivated him to take on the quirky adventure. Using glasses with rear-view mirrors to see traffic, his goal was to walk the world backwards. But Turkish police prevented him from continuing on 24 October 1932.

Wingo had covered an average of 16 miles (25km) each day, supporting himself by selling postcards. He totalled 517 days and 8,000 miles (12,875km). When he returned the Great Depression had worsened and his wife, having pleaded with him to quit the project and return home, had divorced him.

It may or may not have been a consolation to enter the *Guinness Book of World Records* as the greatest exponent of reverse pedestrianism.

24

The fastest marathon in orbit
(16 April 2007)

The Guinness World Record for the fastest marathon in orbit was run by 41-year-old American astronaut Sunita Williams on this day. Williams ran her 26.2 miles (42km) in 4:24, while orbiting Earth on board the International Space Station.

She's from Boston and has previously run the city's famous race – and was competing as an official entrant in the 2007 version. While the race is famed for its atmosphere, Williams had none at all – the weightless runner was strapped to a treadmill with a bungee cord to hold her down. The astronaut circled the Earth at least twice in the process, running as fast as 8mph (12.8km/h), but flying more than 5 miles (8km) each second.

Williams also holds the record for total spacewalks by a woman – seven – and for the most spacewalk time for a woman, with 50 hours and 40 minutes.

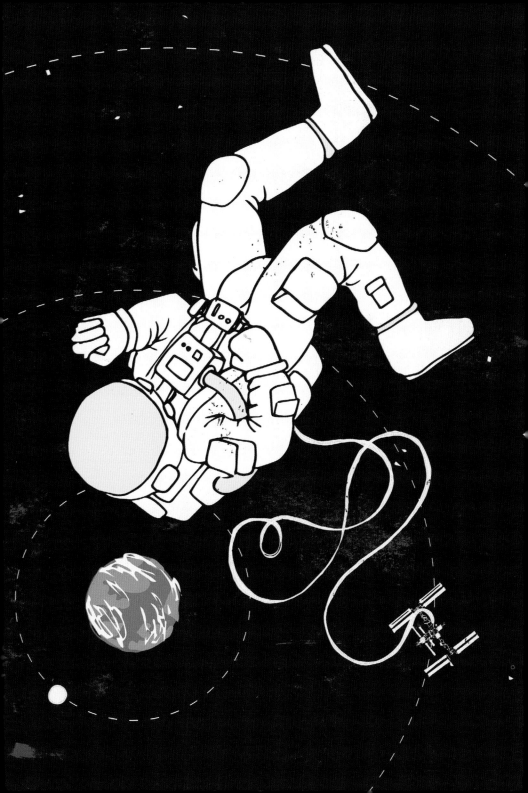

25

Bruce Tulloh runs across America
(20 April 1969)

Not long after British middle-distance runner Bruce Tulloh retired he was flicking through his son's *Guinness Book of Records* and he noticed the record for running across America was 73 days for around 3,000 miles (4,800km). 'I thought, "That should be easy,"' he's said. 'But of course it wasn't.'

The 1962 5,000m European gold medallist and barefoot runner (though he wore shoes for this) set off from Los Angeles. Despite intensive training, he developed 'the most violent cramps' in his thighs after just 24 miles (39km) and injury bedevilled much of his attempt.

Notwithstanding a four-day spell when he was not only reduced to walking, but even resorted to using a walking stick, Tulloh completed the 2,876 miles (4,628km) in just under 65 days, beating the record by eight and a half days. 'It was a very exciting time. Sometimes very tough. Sometimes quite boring. Forrest Gump got the credit for it. I only did it once. He did it two and a half times.'

The record has been broken six times since.

26

The fastest marathon by a vegetable
(22 April 2012)

The Guinness World Record for the fastest marathon run dressed as a jester is 3:01:56, by Switzerland's Alexander Scherz at the 2012 London Marathon, run on this day.

It was a particularly fine year for costume-related world records at the famous UK race. It was also the location for fastest marathon on stilts (6:50:02), wearing an operational gas mask, in a wedding dress, the obligatory man dressed as a fairy, and in a nurse's uniform, dressed as a Roman soldier, a vegetable (male and female records – both carrots), a baby, a nun, a monk, in a two-person pantomime costume, a book character (Dracula), as an insect (bee), hula-hooping, dribbling a football, and the fastest marathon run by a dairy product (ice cream).

27

The longest continuous run
(3 May 2000)

One week into his run around Australia, 50 year-old Gary Parsons had became fully aware of the daunting task ahead.

He was not meant to be doing this. The Australian had been warned by an orthopaedic surgeon that if he ran more than 8 miles (5km) he would end up in a wheelchair. Indeed he took a walking frame with him and would sometimes use it for 30 minutes at the end of the day, when his back felt sore.

On his 274-day adventure Parsons also dealt with unexpected crew departures, vehicle breakdowns, plagues of flies, huge dust clouds and hundreds of kilometres of isolation. Going anticlockwise, from Perth he ran with a stress fracture in his leg.

But when Parsons limped into Brisbane with a badly injured ankle after averaging 45 miles (72.4km) a day for more than nine months he had set a world record for the longest continuous run. He'd clocked up 11,825 miles (19,030km), breaking the previous world record of 10,607 miles (17,071km) set by American Robert Sweetgall in 1983.

'It was my goal to run further than anyone in the history of running,' Parsons told Reuters. 'I guess it is just a bit of Aussie spirit, like the old explorers who went into the beyond and went that bit further.'

He wore out 12 pairs of running shoes during his self-powered quest.

28

Patrick Fitzgerald uses a 'sacrificator'
(4 May 1884)

Six-day racing could make a pedestrian very sleepy. Popular stay-awake remedies included hot baths, plunging one's head into a bucket of ice water, loud music and even electric shocks. At a six-day race at New York's Madison Square in 1884 in front of 12,000 spectators, race leader Patrick Fitzgerald took things a stage further.

His effort to get past the famous Charles Rowell had come back to bite him and lethargy was kicking in, threatening to undo his hard work. His lead of 20 miles (32km) slipped to 10 (16km) on the final day. In desperation a doctor was called for and Dr Naylor arrived with a 'sacrificator', a 'rectangular bronze instrument' with '16 retractable razor-sharp blades', reports *Running Through the Ages*. It was placed on Fitzgerald's thighs and a trigger pulled, slashing the fatigued pedestrian 16 times on each quad muscle.

With leg pressure eased, a revived Fitzgerald went on to set a world record of 610 miles (982km). Yet oddly the sacrificator never really caught on.

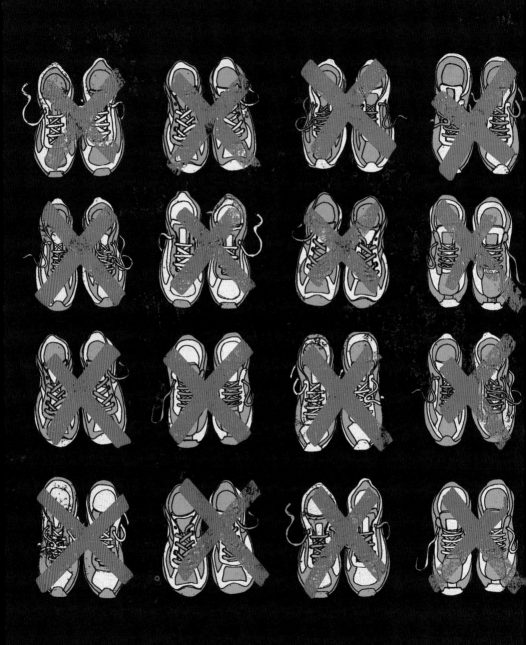

29

Born to Run is published
(5 May 2009)

Born to Run: A Hidden Tribe, Superathletes, and the Greatest Race the World Has Never Seen, written by the American author and journalist Christopher McDougall, has sold three million copies and is the world's most popular running book.

The narrative follows McDougall's attempts to track down members of a reclusive ultramarathon-running tribe, Mexico's Tarahumara, along with the elusive and enigmatic Caballo Blanco.

As well as introducing the wider world to US ultra running legends Scott Jurek, Ann Trason and Jenn Shelton, *Born to Run* was highly critical of the running shoe industry. McDougall argued that modern cushioned running-shoes are a major cause of running injury – a claim which led to the contemporary barefoot running movement.

Rumours persist that the book is being made into a Hollywood film.

30

A race to pick up stones
(14 May 1837)

The first half of the 1800s brought some enterprising variations on pedestrian racing, and races to collect stones were *de rigueur* for a time in the UK – in the US potatoes were sometimes used. Objects would be placed every yard on a straight line for the runner to collect and return to the start to place in a bucket.

On this date, a race to pick up 300 stones – meaning a total race distance of 51.3 miles (82.5km) – saw John Phipps Townsend, who had won the first London to Brighton Race and humbly called himself 'The Champion of Living Pedestrians', competing against the less distinguished Edward 'Temperance' Drinkwater. By way of a handicap, reports Edward Sears's *Running Through the Ages*, Townsend had agreed to collect stones using his mouth – and he had specially sought out larger ones from Brighton Beach – while his opponent could use his hands.

Drinkwater went for the nearer stones first, while his more experienced opponent went for varied distances. He lagged behind Drinkwater for most of the race, but after eight hours Drinkwater gave up, citing exhaustion, and had to be carried to his room. Townsend picked up his last stone, and the win, after 8 hours and 19 minutes.

His party trick was to stand for long periods on one leg, which he once managed for over seven hours. He was forced to retire from pedestrianism when he lost the use of a leg, which may not be entirely coincidental.

31

Grete Waitz sets half marathon record
(15 May 1982)

Grete Waitz ran the Gothenburg half marathon in a world-record time of 1:09:57 on this date. But it was the Norwegian's marathon running that left such a huge mark on athletics history. An unprecedented nine New York City Marathon wins (between 1978 and 1988) included setting world records three years in a row. Overall she lowered the women's world record by nine minutes, taking it from 2:34:47 to 2:25:29, and set various other world records at shorter distances.

Her first marathon, the 1978 New York win, was run after the encouragement of her husband and coach, who told her a trip to New York would be like a second honeymoon for them. The furthest she'd run in training was 13 miles (21km) and she has said the last 10 miles (16km) of the race were agony. Waitz was so angry at her husband at the finish line that she tore off her shoes and flung them at him, yelling, 'I'll never do this stupid thing again!'

In Norway there are statues created in Waitz's honour and she's been depicted on stamps and aeroplanes. Her success has clear parallels with the increased popularity of women running marathons.

32

Sumie Inagaki runs for 48 hours non-stop
(21 May 2010)

Sumie Inagaki had already won Greece's 153-mile (246km) Spartathlon ultramarathon and set a women's 24-hour (indoor) world record, when she attempted a new women's 48-hour (track) record in Surgères, France. So to the casual observer it wasn't a huge surprise when the Japanese distance runner clocked a world best 247 miles (397km) two days later.

Inagaki is also two-time winner of the IAU 24-Hour World Championships. Indeed, the yoga teacher clearly likes to do things twice, as she also won America's notorious Badwater Ultramarathon in 2011 and 2012. She continues to race – and almost always wins – 24- and 48-hour races.

33

First Comrades 'Marathon' run
(24 May 1921)

While serving during World War I with the South African infantry in what is now Tanzania, British-born Vic Clapham and his fellow soldiers marched over 1,678 miles (2,700km). In the aftermath of the war he looked for ways to commemorate the soldiers' suffering and their camaraderie. Inspired by England's 55-mile (88km) London–Brighton ultramarathon, his idea was a 56-mile (90km) race between Pietermaritzburg and Durban in South Africa.

Thanks in part to a £1 loan, the first Comrades Marathon was born on this date, to 'celebrate mankind's spirit over adversity'.

It's not one of the most popular ultramarathons on the planet, with around 20,000 runners – but, as the London–Brighton wasn't yet a regular fixture, it claims to be the oldest.

Uniquely the race changes direction every year, one being the 'up', the other the 'down', reflecting the change in elevation.

The event is renowned for its infectious atmosphere, and the likes of Arthur Newton, Wally Hayward, Hardy Ballington, Jackie Meckler, Alan Robb, nine-time winner Bruce Fordyce, and Russian twins Olesya and Elena Nurgalieva have all become part of Comrades folklore. So too have the near-identical Motsoeneng brothers, repeatedly swapping places during the 1999 race. Their cheating was proved by TV footage showing they were wearing watches on different wrists.

34

The Great Wall Marathon
(27 May 1999)

At most marathons, runners dread hitting The Wall, but at this one contact with a huge stone structure is guaranteed – for 2 miles (3km) along the World Heritage-listed Great Wall of China.

The 5,164 stone steps mean you don't see so many elite Kenyan runners at this one. The route starts near the village of Huangyaguan, a couple of hours northeast of Beijing, and *Runner's World* magazine describes it as a 'relentless series of climbs and descents; a mixture of

small, shallow steps, and painful, knee-high ones'. The temperature can be well above 30° Celsius and the course record is 3:09:18.

The Great Wall Marathon is not to be confused with The Great Wall of China Marathon (also called the Conquer the Wall Marathon), a newer event which takes place in the same month but on a different part of the Great Wall. It claims to be on a more remote section, much of it unrestored since 1570, and includes over 20,000 steps.

35

Pre's last drive
(30 May 1975)

The very promising career of America's Steve Prefontaine ended in a tragic car crash today in 1975. At just 24 'Pre' held the US record in seven distances from 2,000m to 10,000m and seemed a shoo-in for gold medals at the following year's Olympics.

He had placed fourth in the 1972 Olympic 5,000m final, regarded by many as one of the greatest ever races, and is the subject of two Hollywood films, two documentaries and at least four books. Pre had an eye for a quote to rival Muhammad Ali, with his best two being: 'To give anything less than your best, is to sacrifice the gift,' and: 'I'm going to work so that it's a pure guts race at the end, and if it is, I am the only one who can win it.'

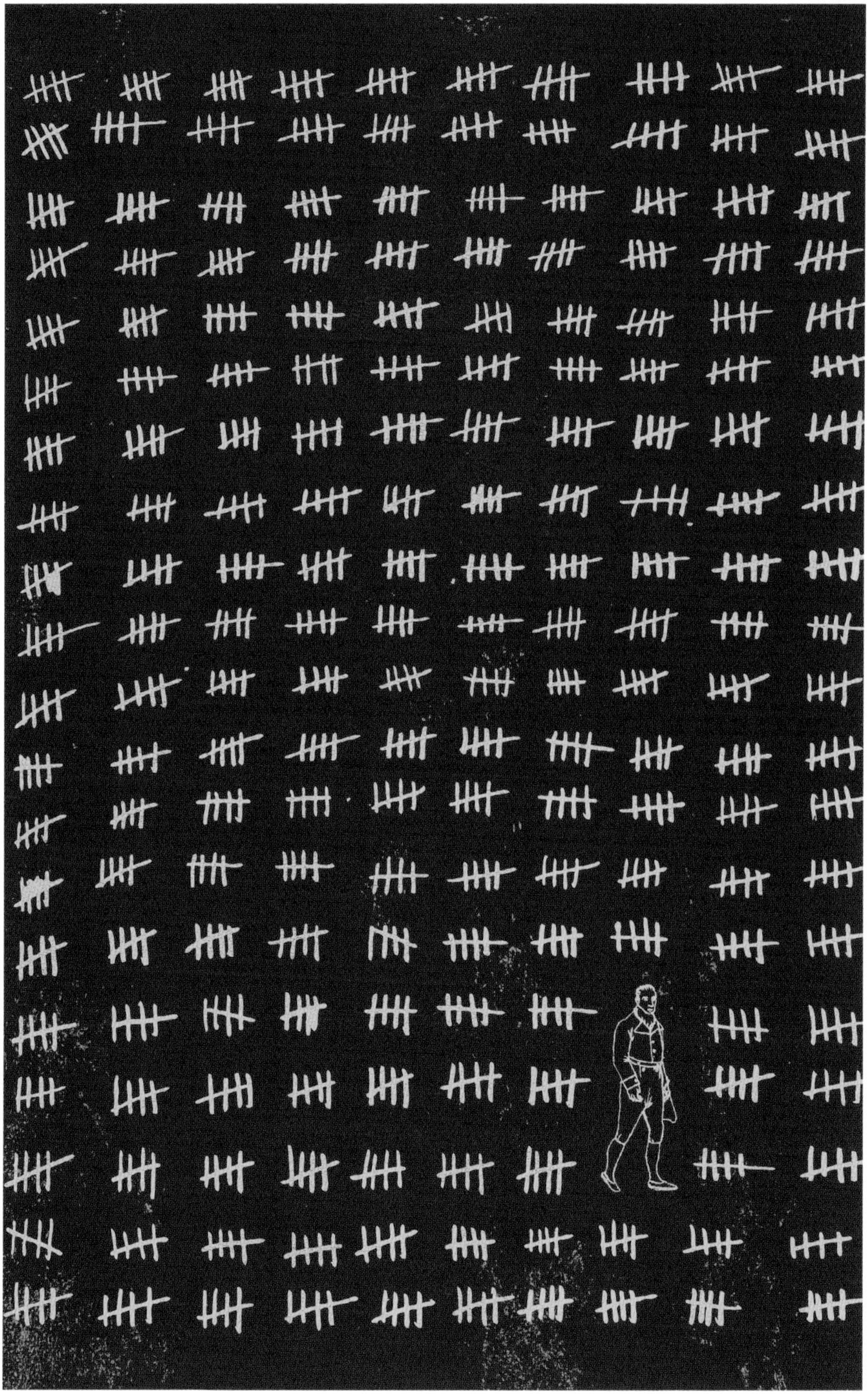

36

The 1,000-mile walk
(1 June 1809)

Scotland's Robert Barclay Allardyce began his walk of 1,000 miles (1,610km) in 1,000 hours for 1,000 guineas today in 1809. 'Captain Barclay', or the 'celebrated pedestrian' as he was also known, was the first great pedestrian of the nineteenth century.

Pedestrianism was the eighteenth- and nineteenth-century feat of walking and/or running seemingly impossible distances, usually for a considerable wager. It was the origin of both racewalking and ultramarathon running.

Walking the equivalent of 24 miles (39km) per day sounds easy, but Barclay had pledged to walk at least a mile (1.6) every hour for 42 days. Around 10,000 spectators gathered at a half-mile (0.8km) course in Newmarket, England. Total betting reached £100,000 (£40m in today's money).

Barclay's sage strategy was to walk a mile at the end of each hour, then another one straight after, at the start of the next hour, allowing himself maximum rest before the next one. Predictably the 29-year-old's pace decreased from just under 15-minute miles at the start to around 21-minute miles. His weight dropped from 13st 4lb (84.5kg) to 11st (70kg). A spectator reported that Barclay become so lethargic that helpers stuck needles in him and even fired pistols close to his ears to try and keep him awake. But he got there to cement his place as the forefather of the pedestrian movement.

37

Thomas Longboat is born
(4 June 1887)

This date is Thomas Longboat day in Canada. It marks the birth of one of the world's great distance runners. Longboat was a Canadian Onondaga Indian who grew up working on a ranch, chasing runaway horses.

Longboat won the 1907 Boston Marathon (then a 24½-mile/39km course) in a record time of 2:24:24 and the following year represented his country at the first Olympic marathon, in London, where he was a favourite. He collapsed, however, as did several leading runners on a hot day (though there were also rumours he'd been drugged).

A rematch was organised between Longboat and Italy's Dorando Pietri at Madison Square Garden, New York, in the same year. Interest was huge and thousands were turned away. Pietri went haring off from the start, but was in a state of collapse on 25 miles (40km), when Longboat sauntered casually past him. They raced again at the same venue the following year, with the same outcome, in comically similar circumstances.

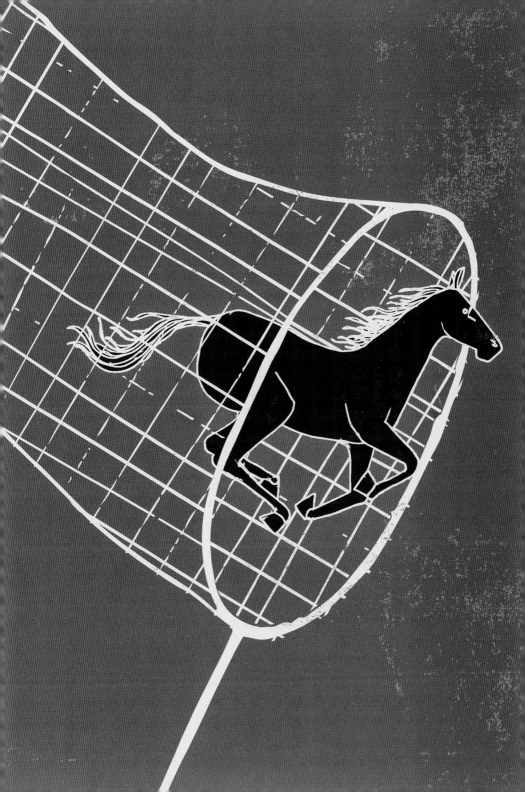

38

Haile Gebrselassie breaks yet another world record
(5 June 1995)

Like Thomas Longboat, Haile Gebrselassie grew up chasing horses and it showed. 1995 saw the great distance runner at his electrifying peak. In May he broke the 2-mile (3.2km) world record, with 8:07.46. In August he won the 10,000m World Championships. Just after that he reclaimed his 5,000m world record, chipping nearly 11 seconds off,

with 12:44.39. And in between all those achievements that would cap most careers the Ethiopian broke the 10,000m world record on 5 June, rocketing to 26:43.53 at Hengelo, Netherlands.

When he retired from competitive running in May 2015, Gebrselassie had claimed two Olympic golds and eight World Championship wins, and set 27 world records. Many see him as the biggest rival to Emil Zátopek as the world's greatest ever distance runner.

39

The Barkley Marathons
(10 June 1977)

When Martin Luther King Jr's murderer James Earl Ray escaped from Brushy Mountain State Penitentiary in Tennessee on 10 June, it didn't become a great foot journey – quite the opposite – but it gave birth to one, namely the world's toughest, and quirkiest, 100-mile (161km) race.

After running for 55 hours, Earl Ray had only travelled 8 miles (13km) through the densely wooded terrain when he was captured. On hearing this, ultrarunner Gary Cantrell thought he could do better and the Barkley Marathon was born.

Since its inception in 1986, only 14 runners out of around 800 have completed it (two more people have walked on the moon, as of 2016). The race, a series of 20-mile (32km) loops, has 54,200 feet (16,520m) of accumulated vertical climb, the equivalent of climbing Mount Everest twice from sea level.

Competitors must find around 10 books and remove the page corresponding to their race number. Failure to produce these at the finish means disqualification. The books often have titles such as *A Time to Die* and that sardonic humour permeates the idiosyncratic event.

'There is no website,' said Cantrell, 'and I don't publish the race date or how to enter.' Potential entrants must write an essay on 'Why I Should Be Allowed to Run in the Barkley', though it's not clear where to send it to. Or when.

The only thing Barkley isn't tough on is your wallet. It costs $1.60 to enter.

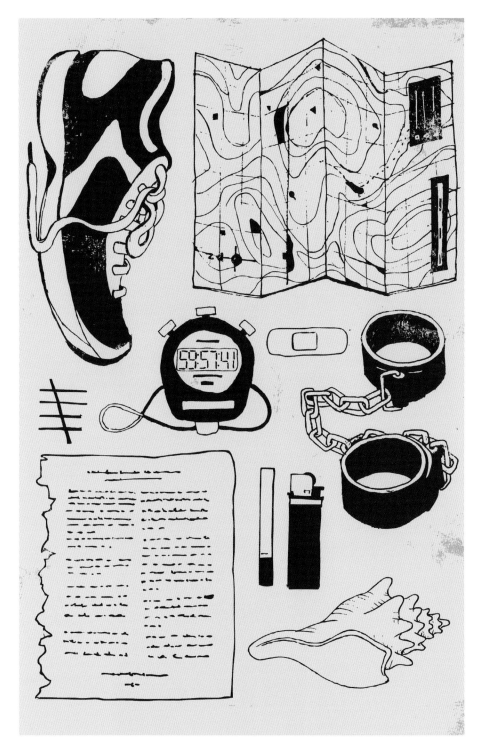

40

Henry Rono breaks the 10,000m world record
(11 June 1978)

An incredible 81-day sequence saw Henry Rono break four world records in 1978: the 10,000m on 11 June in 27:22.5; the 5,000m in 13:08.4; the 3,000m steeplechase in 8:05.4; and the 3,000m in 7:32.1.

He also won the 5,000m and the 3,000m steeplechase gold medals at the Commonwealth Games in the same year. It's a hot streak unparalleled in the history of distance running.

Rono would also set a new world record for 5,000m in 1981.

Sadly, the Kenyan would never get to compete at the Olympics: his country boycotted both the 1976 and the 1980 Games and by 1984 he was no longer competing.

His 3,000m steeplechase world record stood for 11 years.

41

The world's longest race
(16 June 1997)

In 1964, Indian guru Sri Chinmoy moved to New York and started teaching meditation, including running to attain enlightenment. In 1996 he created a 2,700-mile (4,345km) race around a block in New York, but he clearly felt that wasn't testing enough because at the award ceremony he declared the 1997 edition would be extended to 3,100 miles (4,989km). The Self-Transcendence 3,100-Mile Race is the world's longest certified footrace.

From then onwards, runners have undergone 5,649 laps of one extended city block in Queens – they must average 59.62 miles (96km) per day to finish within the 52-day limit.

Participation is limited to invited athletes who have a résumé of multi-day running experience and elite endurance abilities. In the 18 years to 2015, just 37 people completed the distance.

Though it's not a prerequisite for participation, most of the event's competitors are followers of the late Chinmoy. The leader lived about a mile (1.6km) from the race's course until he died in 2007.

According to his website, Sri Chinmoy 'felt that peace could be manifested through silent meditation, music, poetry, art and sports. He especially had a fondness for running and felt it provided an excellent opportunity for people to challenge themselves and overcome their pre-conceived limitations – what he referred to as self-transcendence.'

42

Timothy Olson wins Western States
(23 June 2012)

As well as being the oldest, along with UTMB, the Western States Endurance Run is the world's most competitive 100-mile (161km) race. Starting in Squaw Valley, California, it ends 100.2 miles later in Auburn. Runners climb more than 18,000ft (5,480m) and descend nearly 23,000ft (70,000m) but it is seen as a comparatively fast and runable course.

The legendary Scott Jurek may have won Western States seven consecutive times (see pages 96–7), Tim Twietmeyer five times and Ann Trason 14 times, but it's Timothy Olson, with his trademark long hair and beard, who has the course record.

He was the first runner to break 15 hours, clocking 14:46:44 in 2012. Olson won again the following year, but in a slower time.

Olson initially took to running cross country to get in shape for basketball, but he found the sport, and runners, to be more to his liking. He went off the rails at college, turning to drink and drugs, but thankfully he rediscovered running and says it may well have saved his life.

43

Ernst arrives in Moscow
(25 June 1832)

Norway's Mensen Ernst, famous pedestrian and godfather of ultramarathon running, arrived in Moscow today in 1832, two days ahead of schedule, having travelled on foot from Paris in just 14 days, the first of his three epic trips.

But hold on a minute. The distance from Paris to Moscow, as the crow flies, is 1,500 miles (2,414km), so that's 107 miles (172km) per day. An averagely fit ultramarathon runner nowadays could maybe cover 107 miles in 20 hours, but they'd need a good old sleep – certainly more than four hours – before doing it all the next day. Norwegian author Bredo Berntsen has found numerous flaws in claims made about Ernst in his biography *Des Stauermannes Mensen Ernst.*

However, some newspaper reports from the time do support aspects of Ernst's second big journey, from Germany to Greece. 'We can't dismiss Ernst outright,' writes Edward S. Sears in the excellent *Running Through the Ages.* 'He was at the very least a popular and colourful long-distance pedestrian.'

44

Rookie Scott Jurek wins Western States
(26 June 1999)

Scott Jurek is America's greatest ultra runner, but he hated running at first. He began purely as cross-training for the ski season. Everything changed for him in 1994, when Jurek ran his first Minnesota Voyageur 50-miler (80km) ultramarathon. He placed second and discovered a hidden taste for ultra-distance races.

In 1999 he was on the start line for Western States, the most prestigious 100-miler (160km-er) in the US, if not the world. He led

from start to finish. It would be the first of an unprecedented seven consecutive wins.

The American has also won the 153-mile (246km) Spartathlon three consecutive times, the 135-mile (217km) Badwater Ultramarathon twice, the Hardrock 100 and many other races, with numerous course records along the way.

Jurek is known for his veganism, his primal howls on the start line and staying at the finish line to clap home the rest of the field.

45

Running around the world
(1 July 2008)

Danish political scientist Jesper Olsen and Australian ultramarathon runner Sarah Barnett set off from Norway today to run around the world.

Olsen, who held various national records for ultra running, had already done it once. In 2004–05 he went west–east from London, taking 22 months and making him the second verified person to have run around the globe, covering some 16,000 miles (25,750km).

This time he went via the north–south route – the first known attempt to do so. GPS-tracked all the way, the pair passed through Finland, Denmark, Hungary and Turkey. But on 1 December, in Turkey, after 4,557 miles (7,334km), Barnett had to give up.

Olsen continued alone through Africa, but then had to spend more than six months recovering in Denmark due to dysentery, malaria and two operations to eliminate infections in his right arm.

He continued his run on 1 January 2011 from Punta Arenas, through South America and North America to Newfoundland, finishing at Cape Spear on 28 July 2012 and clocking up 23,000 miles (37,000km).

46

Jules Ladoumègue sets 2,000m world record
(2 July 1931)

During the Great Depression the French needed a star and they found one in middle-distance runner Jules Ladoumègue. The sport enjoyed a huge resurgence, fuelled by newsreel coverage.

In 1928, Ladoumègue started to work with famed coach and Olympic silver medallist Charles Poulenard. He won the 1,500m at the French Championships, qualifying for the 1928 Olympics. Racing hard in the final against two Finns, Eino Purje and Harri Larva, Ladoumègue claimed a laudable second place.

In 1930, after Ladoumègue defeated 1,500m world-record holder Otto Peltzer, he eyed the record of 3:51.0 himself.

With pacers on a Paris track, Ladoumègue not only bagged the record, he became the first sub-3:50 1,500m runner. He went on to set world records for the 1,000m (2:23.6) and 2,000m (5:21.8).Then he broke the mile record, with 4:09.2.

Ladoumègue was a national hero and a big favourite to win gold at the 1932 Los Angeles Olympics. But the French Federation banned him for life because he had allegedly received payments when he was meant to be an amateur. His career was over.

47

The Complete Book of Running is released
(4 July 1977)

When author Jim Fixx started running in 1967 at the age of 35 he weighed 17st 2lb (110kg) and smoked two packs of cigarettes per day. Ten years later, when his book *The Complete Book of Running* was published by Random House, he was 4st 4lb (27kg) lighter and smoke-free.

The book spent 11 weeks on the top of the best-seller list and is credited with kick-starting America's fitness revolution, popularising running and demonstrating the health benefits of regular jogging.

As well as the physical benefits of running, *The Complete Book of Running* discusses its psychological benefits: increasing self-esteem, acquiring a 'high' from running, and being able to cope better with pressure and tension.

Ironically and tragically, Fixx died of a heart attack, aged 52, while jogging, giving plenty of ammunition for anti-running barflys the world over. In fact he died from a congenital heart disease. His father had his first heart attack at 35 and died of another at 43.

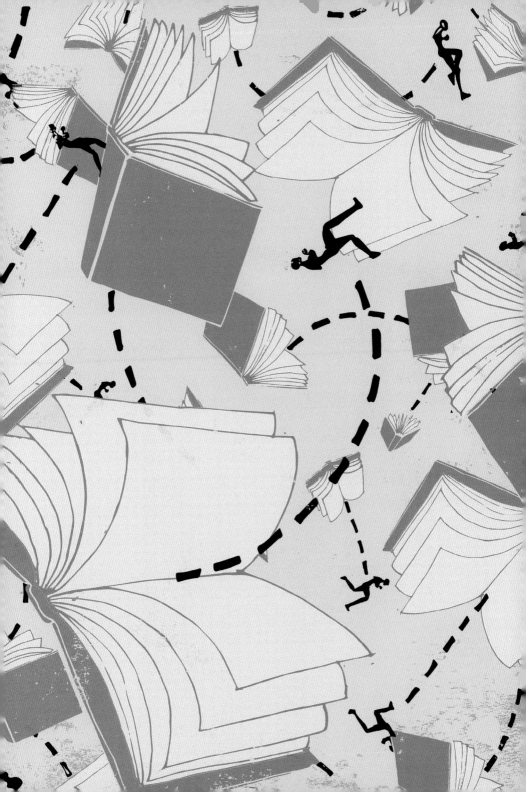

48

Hannes Kolehmainen wins three Olympic golds
(7 July 1912)

Finnish distance runner Hannes Kolehmainen, nicknamed 'Smiling Hannes' because of his perpetually happy face, was vegetarian, and a bricklayer by trade, but more notably the first great distance runner of the Olympic Games. He was one of the 'Flying Finns' who dominated the track in the early twentieth century.

Kolehmainen's success predated the peerless Paavo Nurmi and his biggest success was the 1912 Olympics in Stockholm. From his first heat, on 7 July, in the 10,000m, he went on to win three gold medals: for 5,000m, 10,000m and in Cross Country. The 5,000m final was the most memorable.

World War I almost certainly came between Kolehmainen and further success and after it he switched to the roads. He finished fourth in the 1917 Boston Marathon, and won another Olympic gold in the 1920 marathon final at Antwerp. Later he set world records at both 25km and 30km.

49

London's 'Austerity Games'
(29 July 1948)

The post-World War II 'Austerity Games' in London cost just £730,000 to put on. No new venues or an Olympic village were built, and Olympians were encouraged to buy or make their own uniforms, though they were allowed extra food rations.

The Netherlands' Fanny Blankers-Koen was one of the big stories. Known as the 'Flying Housewife', the 30-year-old mother of three took home four gold medals (for the 100m, 200m, 80m hurdles and 4x100m relay).

The world also saw the emergence of Emil Zátopek. In the 10,000m final the Czech lapped all but two runners, winning by more than 330 yards/300m. In the 5,000m final he was trailing by 55 yards/50m at the start of the final lap but closed the gap with a sensational sprint, though he still had to settle for silver, finishing just behind Belgium's Gaston Etienne Reiff.

50

Delany–Ibbotson rematch
(30 July 1957)

Irishman Ron Delany's 1,500m win at the 1956 Melbourne Olympics was a sensation. He had only been running seriously for four years, had beaten local favourite John Landy in an Olympic record time, and was the first Irishman to win an Olympic medal for over 20 years.

Over four seasons (1956–59) he was unbeaten in 40 indoor races in the US – one of the greatest winning streaks of all time. He set several Irish records and also beat the world indoor mile record three times, reducing it to 4:01.4.

But in July 1957, Delany raced in the Amateur Athletic Association 880 yards in London and won. In the mile race he finished second to Derek Ibbotson, who broke the world record.

Ten days later, on 30 July, Ibbotson faced Delany in a rematch in Ireland and a chance for revenge. According to Delany, the 25,000-strong home crowd were 'deranged, distracted and almost dancing with hysterical delight' over his victory against the new world record holder.

51

The first Badwater ultramarathon
(31 July 1987)

America's Badwater ultramarathon is hardly alone in claiming to be the hardest or most extreme event around. But it has a worthy claim.

The initial concept was a race between the lowest and highest points in the contiguous US: from the Badwater Basin in California's Death Valley to Mount Whitney's summit, at 14,505ft (4,421m).

The two points are only 80 miles (129km) apart on the map. But because of detours, around lake beds and over mountain ranges, the distance on land is some 146 miles (235km).

Due to the two mountain ranges that must be crossed, the course's cumulative elevation gain exceeds 19,000ft (6,000m). But neither of these two challenges are what the event is most notorious for. The race takes place annually in mid-July, when temperatures over 49°C (120°F), even in the shade, aren't uncommon.

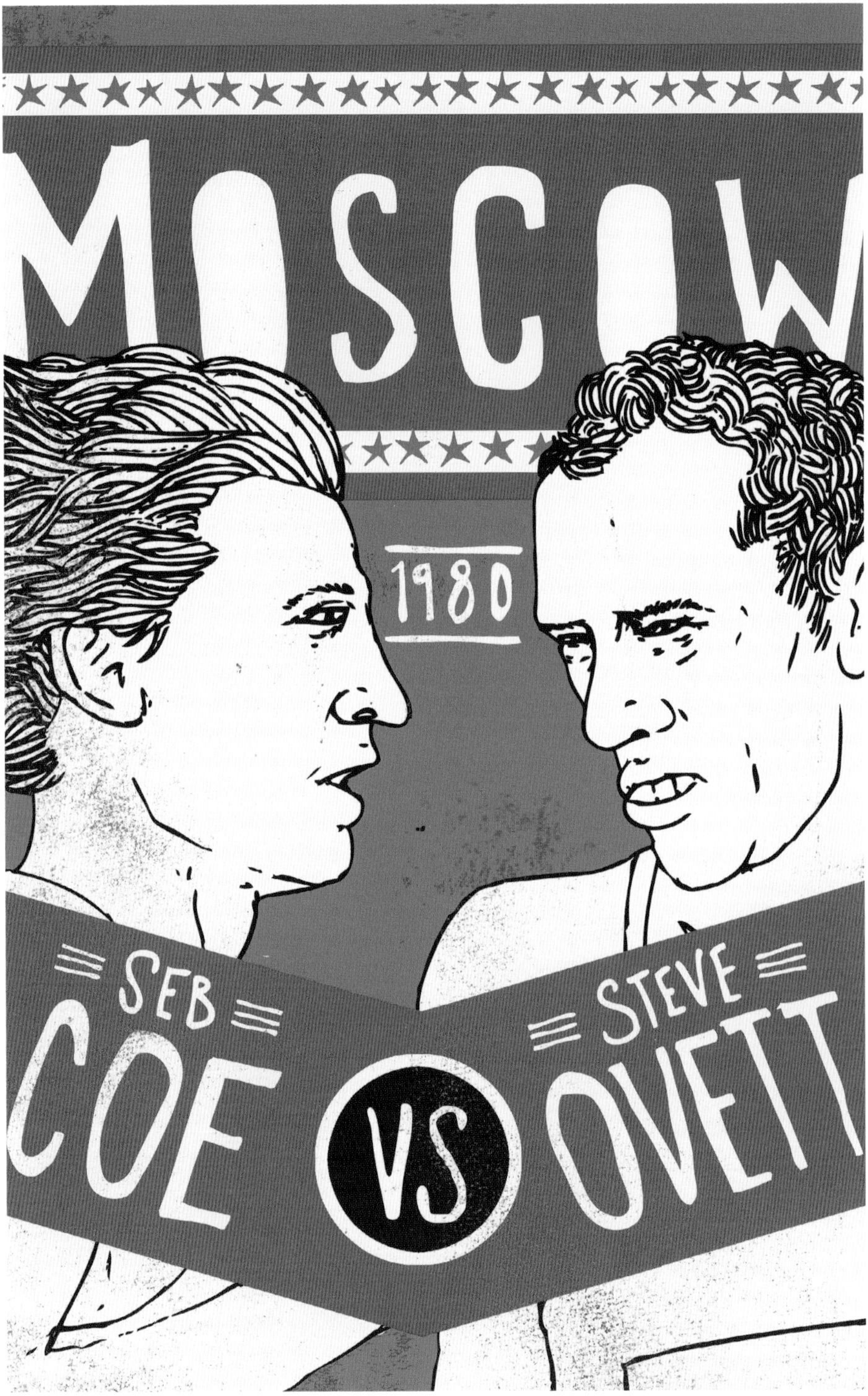

MOSCOW
1980
SEB
COE
VS
STEVE
OVETT

52

Steve Ovett versus Seb Coe
(1 August 1980)

Britons Steve Ovett and Seb Coe were the world's two best middle-distance runners of the early 1980's and one of the sport's greatest rivalries.

They were chalk and cheese: Coe favoured the 800m, while Ovett was stronger at 1,500m; Coe was from the north of England, Ovett from the south coast; Coe was the more driven, Ovett the more relaxed; Coe was seen as an establishment figure, Ovett more of a rebel. Ovett was reluctant to play the press game, while future politician and IAAF president Coe was far more accessible.

Coming into the 1980 Olympics, Coe had broken three world revords in 41 days. However, in the Olympic 800m he got his tactics horribly wrong. He got boxed in and left it too late to make a move. Ovett finished three yards in front, with gold. Despite gaining silver, Coe called the race 'the very worst 800 metres of my 20-year career'.

Six days later they met again in the 1,500m final. Coe wasn't going to get boxed in this time. Around the final bend, he kicked past East German Jürgen Straub to come home 4 yards (3.6m) clear. Ovett took bronze. Each had won the event they were thought to be weaker at. For such a big rivalry, the pair rarely raced directly. They only met six times in their entire careers, with four of those meetings coming in Olympic finals.

53

Mo's magic moment
(4 August 2012)

The Olympic 10,000m final had been won by an African at every Games since 1984. A British runner had never won a 10,000m or 5,000m gold. Though Somalia-born, Mo Farah moved to London aged eight and at the 2008 Beijing Olympics he had failed to qualify for the 5,000m final. He moved to Oregon, US, and started working with maverick Cuba-born coach Alberto Salaza, running 120 miles (193km) a week and training at the same high-altitude camps as his Kenyan opponents. He became world champion, so expectation was huge for his home London Games.

Ethiopian Kenenisa Bekele, reigning Olympic 5,000m and 10,000m champion, led initially, with Farah waiting patiently. With five laps left, Farah slipped into third behind Kenyan Moses Masai and Tariku Bekele, Kenenisa's brother.

Crowd noise grew, urging Farah to take the lead, but he showed studied discipline. The leading pack jostled for position. As tension rose, with 500m/547 yards to go, he finally hit the front. No one could match his kick, and he crossed the line in 27:30:42. 'This is the best moment of my life,' said an emotional Farah.

54

A controversial race that got even more controversial
(11 August 1984)

Few races had been as talked about beforehand as the 1984 Olympic 3,000m final. Zola Budd had deserted South Africa, the country where she was born which was banned from Olympic competition due to its apartheid regime, for Britain. Her citizenship, available due to British grandparents, was controversially fast-tracked. Anti-apartheid activists were unhappy and her first race meet as a Briton was cancelled at short notice.

Budd, who ran barefoot, had broken the women's 5,000m world record aged just 17 and most expected gold to go to her or American world champion Mary Decker.

Decker set off at a fast pace, but Budd took over on halfway. At 1,700m (1,870 yards), running in a pack, Decker came into contact with one of Budd's legs, knocking her slightly off balance. Not long after Budd's foot brushed Decker's thigh, causing Budd to lose balance and tumble into Decker's path. Decker's spikes came down into Budd's ankle, drawing blood. Budd kept her stride, but an off-balance Decker fell onto the infield, tearing off Budd's number. She was out of the race with a hip injury.

Budd continued to lead, but faded, finishing seventh, well outside her best time, as the crowd booed. Later she said she slowed as she couldn't face collecting a medal in front of the disapproving crowd. An IAAF jury found her not responsible for the collision.

55

Racing footmen
(14 August 1660)

It was fashionable for sixteenth-century Turkish nobleman to have couriers, or runner messengers. The Grand Turk was said to have between 80 and 100 *peirles* (lackeys or footmen), usually from Persia and often in jester-esque uniforms, including jangling bells. In *Wonders of Bodily Strength and Skill,* Guillaume Depping tells of one running 120 miles (193km) in 24 hours – they were the forefathers of the pedestrian movement.

The trend spread across western Europe in the seventeenth and eighteenth centuries, when they were often used to run ahead of carriages to look for hazards on the rudimentary (i.e. potholed) roads. Sixty miles (96km) in a day wasn't uncommon.

Noblemen took pride in the running ability of their footmen, arranging races and betting heavily. We don't know when the first footmen race was, but as of 1660, three times around London's Hyde Park was certainly a fixture each August.

A spate of footmen dying from 'consumption' (tuberculosis) after three to four years breathing in germ-laden air on the dusty roads may have led to the commonly held idea at the time, even by doctors, that running was bad for you.

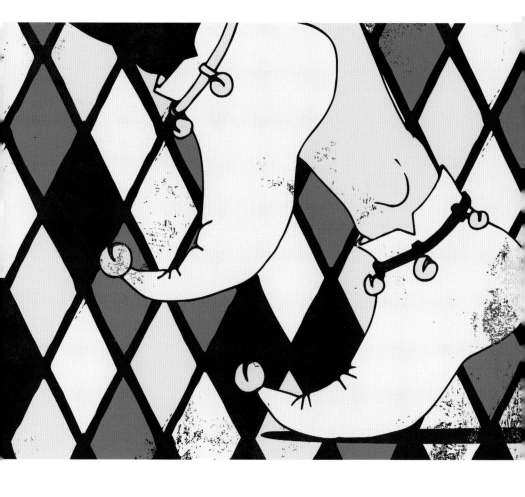

56

Joseph Guillemot shocks Paavo Nurmi
(17 August 1920)

The 1920 Olympic 5,000m final is remarkable in that Finland's Paavo Nurmi didn't win it. The Flying Finn won three other golds at these Games, but he only finished second here as Joseph Guillemot beat him. The Frenchman's victory was all the more impressive as his lungs had been severely damaged by mustard gas in World War I, his heart was located on the right side of his chest and he was a pack-a-day smoker.

Nurmi had tried to exhaust his two main rivals, the Swedes Eric Backman and Rudolf Falk, and after three laps only Guillemot was still with the Finn. On the final curve the Frenchman overtook the tiring Nurmi, finishing over four seconds ahead of the runner who would win five golds at the next Olympics, including for 5,000m.

Guillemot had his sights on a double gold, but the 10,000m final was moved forward at the request of Belgium's King Albert – something Joseph only found out at short notice after a large lunch. He battled his bloated belly and shoes two sizes too big to finish second, behind Nurmi. Then he vomited at the awards ceremony.

57

Usain Bolt does the triple
(20 August 2008)

On this date, Usain Bolt won the 2008 Olympic 200m in Beijing's Bird's Nest, with a world-record time of 19.30 seconds, breaking Michael Johnson's 1996 record – and just hours before his twenty-second birthday too.

The nominative determinist had already won 100m gold, breaking his own world record in the process, with 9.69, despite seeming to ease up at the line (and having a shoelace undone).

Then he and his Jamaican team-mates took three-tenths of a second off the best 4x100m time, to make Bolt the first man to win all three events in world-record times.

At the 2012 Olympics he won all three events again.

58

Ultra-Trail du Mont-Blanc
(25 August 2003)

The Ultra-Trail du Mont-Blanc (UTMB) has become Europe's most competitive and popular 100-mile race. Starting and finishing in Chamonix in France, it's equally renowned for its gruelling trails through the French, Italian and Swiss Alps, on the popular Trail du Mont-Blanc hiking trail with a height gain of 32,000 feet (10,000m), as it is for the Eurotrash razzamatazz and relatively 'gourmet' aid stations (well there's more than one type of cheese anyway). Crowds line the trails right up into the mountains, cheering runners on.

While elite runners complete it in around 22 hours, many will take up to 47 hours to return to Chamonix – a heroic feat of stubbornness and endurance. The 2,500-plus places are so popular it could sell out twice over and a ballot system decides places.

Hundred-mile trail ultramarathons have a longer history in the US, but every August the best male runners from across the Atlantic come to France to try and win – and so far, they haven't. American Rory Bosio, however, has won the women's race twice.

59

Egg white and brandy lead to a wobbly athlete
(30 August 1904)

Thomas Hicks won the gold medal in the marathon at the 1904 Olympics in St Louis, USA, despite some dubious nutritional choices. At 18 miles (29km) the British-born American asked for water but received a wet sponge to suck on and, thoughtfully, an egg white. A few miles later, he received two eggs, a sip of brandy and a small dose of strychnine sulphate (considered to be a stimulant at the time but later used as a rat poison).

Over the final 2 miles (3km) of the hilly route he was given two more eggs and two more shots of brandy. He finished the race in first place, though he had to be helped across the finish line and wasn't stable and coherent enough to receive his trophy.

Fred Lorz had crossed the line ahead of him, but had received a lift in a car from mile 9 (km 15) to mile 20 (km 32). When he was disqualified he claimed it was all a joke. Lorz would win the Boston Marathon the following year, apparently fairly.

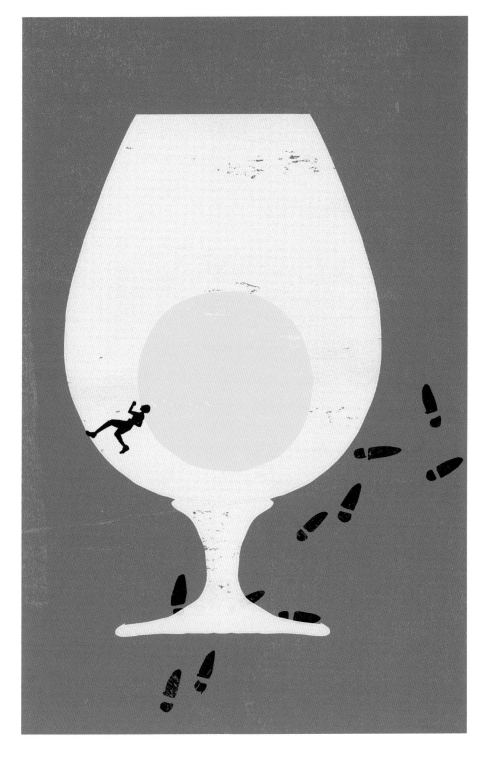

60

The first black African to win Olympic gold
(10 September 1960)

Ethiopia's Abebe Bikila, a member of Emperor Haile Selassie's bodyguard, was a last-minute replacement in the marathon for injured Wami Biratu, boarding the plane to Rome as it was about to leave. In Italy he quickly wore through his one pair of running shoes and a pair donated by Adidas didn't fit well, causing blisters. So he went barefoot, which only added to the widespread view of Bikila as a no-hoper – he was described by one commentator during the race as 'that unknown Ethiopian'.

By 13 miles (20km) only Moroccan Rhadi Ben Abdesselam remained with Bikila. The Ethiopian had been warned that Rhadi, supposed to be wearing number 26, was the one to watch and Bikila spent much of the race searching for his number. But Rhadi was in fact wearing 185 – and could be found right next to him.

As would become his trademark, Bikila increased the pace on 13 miles (20km). Yet it wasn't until the final 550 yards (500m) that he finally pulled away conclusively. Finishing in 2:15:16, Bikila shattered Emil Zátopek's Olympic record by nearly eight minutes.

His victory came less than 25 years after Italian dictator Benito Mussolini had invaded Ethiopia after a brutal colonial war, but also marked the rise of East African middle- and long-distance runners and was the defining moment of the 1960 Olympics.

61

The inaugural New York City Marathon
(13 September 1970)

Now the largest marathon in the world, with 50,304 finishers in 2013 and usually around two million spectators, the New York City Marathon has come a long way. In 1970 just 127 competitors ran several loops around Central Park as about a hundred spectators watched Gary Muhrcke win in 2:31:38.

'I only signed up 15 minutes before the race,' said the 30-year-old New York fireman. 'I hadn't trained for three weeks because of a leg injury, but I felt OK, so I decided to run.' The entry fee of $1 was reflected in the prizes of cheap watches and recycled baseball and bowling trophies.

Nowadays the race takes place in November, is one of the prestigious six World Marathon Majors, and the course travels through the five boroughs of New York City.

62

A marathon drinking session
(14 September 1660)

Held every September in France's Médoc region, near Bordeaux, the Marathon du Médoc may be 26.2 miles (42.2km) long, but that's where the similarity with most other marathons ends.

The route winds through scenic vineyards where, instead of water stations, participants are offered and expected to taste up to 23 glasses of wine – while also stuffing themselves with local specialities such as oysters, foie gras and cheese. Fancy dress is compulsory. The cut-off is a generous six and a half hours and every finisher gets a bottle of wine.

Though it was meant to take place in 1984, the first official race didn't happen until 1985. 'There were some problems with administration – they're very strict about health and safety over here,' said marathon president Vincent Fabre.

63

Dean Karnazes runs 50 marathons in 50 days
(17 September 2006)

American former marketing executive Dean Karnazes began his self-created and much-publicised challenge to run 50 marathons in 50 consecutive days in 50 US states on this day.

Before he set off, Karnazes performed a lactate threshold test in Colorado. 'They said the test would take 15 minutes, tops,' he told the *Guardian*. 'Finally, after an hour, they stopped the test. They said they'd never seen anything like this before.'

The *Ultramarathon Man* author started with the Lewis and Clark Marathon in St Louis and finished with the New York City Marathon on 5 November – clocking 3:00:30. Eight of the runs were conventional marathons, but as most events are on weekends Karnazes ran marathon courses in each state on weekdays.

Karnazes is nearly as famous for arranging for pizzas to be delivered to him mid-run as he is for covering vast distances. He once said, 'There's magic in misery,' and treats blisters by popping them and slathering them with glue.

64

Patrick Makau breaks marathon world record
(25 September 2011)

Kenya's Patrick Makau broke the marathon world record at Berlin running a stunning 2:03:38 (an average pace of 4:42.9 per mile). He also left the legendary Haile Gebrselassie, whose record he trumped by 21 seconds, in his wake at halfway.

'In the morning my body was not good,' he said, 'but after I started the race, it started reacting very well. I started thinking about the record.'

Makau's first marathon, at Rotterdam in 2009, was just 24 seconds short of the fastest ever debut – running 2:06:14. He's a dab hand at half marathons, too, running the second-fastest ever in 2009, of 58:52. He held the marathon world record for two years, creating a bridge from Haile Gebrselassie (2:03:59) to Wilson Kipsang (2:03:23).

The last six marathon world records have been set at Berlin. Not since Khalid Khannouchi's 2:05:38 in London in 2002 has one been run elsewhere.

65

The first female marathon runner?
(29 September 1918)

Rightly or wrongly, neither the IAAF nor the Association of Road Running Statisticians (ARRS) recognises Stamata Revithi as the first woman to run a marathon.

Instead, French runner Marie-Louise Ledru is often credited as the first female to cover the distance, doing so on this date. Ledru reportedly completed the Tour de Paris Marathon in a time of 5:40, finishing in thirty-eighth place. So, a huge moment for both feminism and distance running. But unfortunately things may not be so straightforward.

While the ARRS support Ledru's mark, as usual the IAAF disagrees, instead recognising Britain's Violet Piercy as being the ground-breaking runner, though this has some question marks against it too.

In previous generations the word 'marathon' didn't necessarily mean 26.2 miles (42.2km), rather a 'long road run'. Which is helpful in a way, but unhelpful in that it probably applies to both Ledru's and Piercy's 'marathons'. Either way though, a woman running for well over five hours when it was commonly thought that would be the last thing they'd ever do, deserves our hearty applause.

66

Rosie Swale-Pope heads off around the world
(2 October 2003)

On her fifty-seventh birthday, inspired by her late husband and wanting to raise awareness and funds for cancer, Rosie Swale-Pope left Tenby, Wales, on foot to run around the world.

In Siberia she got frostbite and almost lost her toes. A wolf also popped its head into her tent to say hello. 'He never hurt me and he and his pack followed me for a while,' she said. 'It was like they were running with me.'

Another morning she woke up to find a man coming at her with an axe. She thought he was yelling at her in anger, only to realise he was yelling with joy. He hugged her and invited her to a party with his fellow woodsman.

It took her four years and 10 months, and just under 20,000 miles (32,000km), to circle the world, the writer and adventurer returning home on 25 August 2008.

67

John Foden runs from Athens to Sparta
(9 October 1982)

John Foden, a British RAF Wing Commander and student of Ancient Greek history, reached the statue of Leonidas Sparta, in Sparta, Greece, today in 1982. His experiment had been successful.

Foden had been reading about the battle of Marathon in 490 BC. In Herodotus's account, Athenian messenger Pheidippides is sent to Sparta for reinforcements to help see off the Persian incursion. According to Herodotus, Pheidippides arrived in Sparta, 155 miles (250km) away, a day after departing from Athens. Foden wondered if a modern man could cover the distance within 36 hours. He and four RAF colleagues tried it out. Running a route as close as possible to Herodotus' description, Foden and two of his colleagues made it.

As a result the Spartathlon race, 136 miles (219km) from Marathon to Sparta, was born, with the first event taking place the next year.

The race has since grown to be a major event in the international ultramarathon calendar and the scene of some of the greatest endurance performances ever seen, especially by Yiannis Kouros (see page 33), Scott Jurek (see pages 96–7) and Lizzy Hawker.

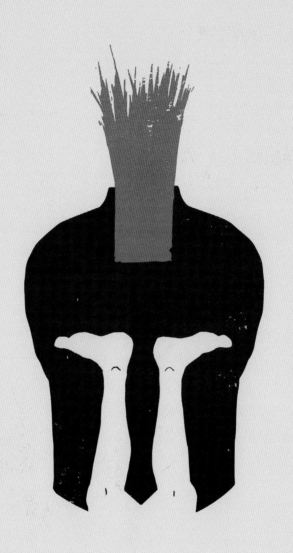

68

Geronimo Jim
(17 October 1964)

Jim Alder set a record on this day for the longest distance covered in a two-hour track race, 23.6 miles (37.994km). But it was bittersweet. He was only there because he hadn't quite made the British marathon team for the 1964 Tokyo Olympics, an event which would be run just four days later.

'I cried in the showers afterwards,' he said. 'You only have these purple-patch days three or four times in your career – running at world-record marathon pace for two hours – while the Olympic marathon was taking place in Tokyo.'

Early life hadn't been kind to him either. His mother died of tuberculosis and his father was killed on the last day of World War II, so he was raised an orphan.

Britain's 1960s distance-running great worked as a bricklayer and would cry out 'Geronimo!' whenever he crossed the finish line, earning himself a nickname. Alder also set a 30,000m record of 1:34:01 and won Commonwealth gold in 1966 for the marathon, his specialist distance – but that almost went very wrong.

Alder arrived at the stadium in Kingston, Jamaica, in the lead but found no officials to guide him into the arena. When he finally made it on to the track, the Scot found England's Bill Adcocks 50 yards (46m) ahead of him, with 300 yards (274m) left. Alder put his head down and charged for the line – as he breasted the tape first he of course bellowed his signature 'Geronimo!'.

69

Emil Zátopek sets world record
(22 October 1949)

Emil Zátopek set a new world record on this day for 10,000m, with 29:21.2 in Ostrava, Czech Republic. With a level of brilliance that was almost tedious, the 'Czech Express' broke his own record the following summer. And again in 1953. Oh, and again in 1954.

He was thought to be the hardest trainer of his era – and it showed – with ideas based loosely on what he'd read about the great Finnish runner Paavo Nurmi, including intervals. 'Why should I practise running slowly?' he said. 'I already know how to run slow.'

Zátopek wasn't just remarkable on the track. Off it he took night classes and would eventually speak six languages. He used his fame to stand up to political bullies too. In the lead-up to the 1952 Helsinki Olympics, Czechoslovakia's Communist Party omitted fellow runner Stanislav Jungwirth from the team because his father was a political prisoner. 'If he does not go, neither do I,' Zátopek declared. The Communists stuck to their word. Zátopek didn't board the plane to Helsinki. The government caved in and sent both runners to the Games.

In 1968, as Russian tanks invaded his homeland, Zátopek openly protested at the intrusion. After Soviet forces had brought a bloody end to the uprising Zátopek was stripped of his rank of colonel, kicked out of the army and forced to collect rubbish on Prague's streets – then spent seven years working in a uranium mine. He was finally pardoned.

70

Boston's first lady, Bobbi Gibb, is born
(2 November 1942)

In 1966 Roberta 'Bobbi' Gibb changed the world by running the Boston Marathon. Before then it was thought that women simply weren't capable of doing such a thing.

She grew up as an active child. 'As soon as you became an adolescent, everything changed,' Gibb told *Women in the World*. She watched the 1964 race. 'Something inside of me said, "I'm going to run this race."' She had applied for a place, but was rejected. Allowing a woman to run 26 miles, the letter said, would be a tremendous liability. 'It wasn't until later that I realised I was going to be making a social statement.'

After three nights and four days travelling on a bus from San Diego, Gibb concealed her face with a hoodie and hid in bushes near the start pen wearing her brother's Bermuda shorts, nurse's shoes (women's running shoes didn't exist then) and no number. When the men rushed by, she jumped from the bushes and into the race. Gibb soon overheated, but didn't want to remove her hoodie and give the game away, however seeing the encouragement from spectators and runners alike, she finally did.

Gibb's feet were covered in blisters and by mile 20 (km 32) she couldn't do much more than tiptoe along. 'I had this huge weight of responsibility on me. Here I was, making this very public statement. If I had collapsed or hadn't finished, I would have set women back another 50 years.' But she placed in the top third of the field.

The Boston Marathon finally opened to women in 1972. Gibb is recognised by the Boston Athletic Association as the pre-sanctioned-era women's winner in 1966, 1967 and 1968.

71

Wrong-way Silva
(6 November 1936)

In the 1994 New York City Marathon, Mexicans Germán Silva and Benjamin Paredes were jockeying for position at the front of the race. But just half a mile (0.8km) from the finish, Silva followed a police vehicle turning right into Central Park, and off-course. He'd gifted his rival a 40-yard (37m) advantage – huge at that stage of a race.

An easy win seemed inevitable for Paredes, but Silva retraced his steps with surprising calmness. He then accelerated, caught his compatriot, passed him and won the race by a few feet. It was going to be a thrilling finish anyway, but this doubled the drama.

Silva came back the next year and won it again, this time without a moment of topographical embarrassment.

He represented Mexico twice at the Olympics in the marathon, and was a silver medallist at the 1994 IAAF World Half Marathon Championships, where he set a Mexican record of 1:00:28.

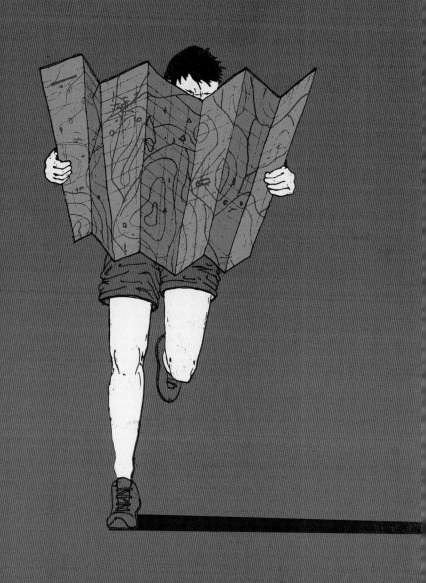

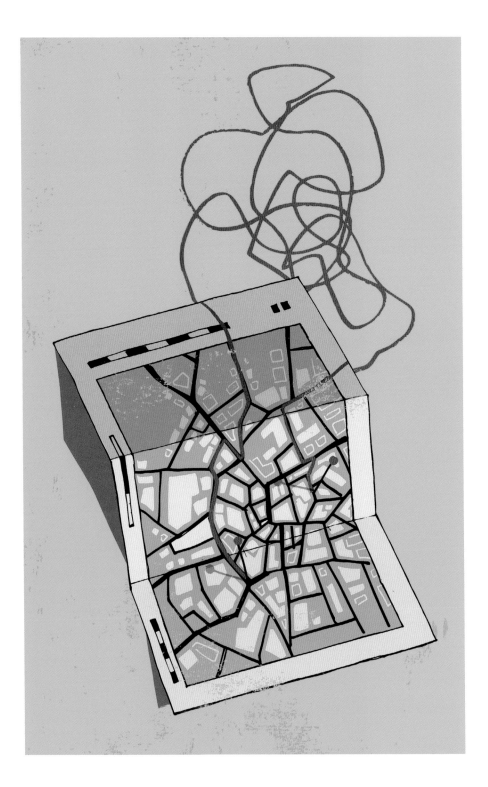

72

Bangkok's 17-mile half marathon
(15 November 2015)

A mishap on this day turned Bangkok's half marathon into the world's longest. A race official responsible for pointing runners in the right direction inadvertently directed them to U-turn at the wrong place. It added more than 2 miles (3km) to each lap and more than 4 miles (6km) to the whole half (and a bit more) marathon.

Despite the bonus miles, making it food value for money and news around the world, some runners voiced annoyance on social media, and organisers 'admitted that a technical error happened during the half-marathon event'.

'The [Jogging Association of Thailand] apologises for the mistake,' vice-president Songrakm Kraison told the Associated Press. 'It will not happen again in the future.'

73

The Marathon Monks of Mount Hiei
(16 November 1885)

The so-called 'marathon monks' are more accurately known as *kaihogyo*, from the Tendai Sect of Buddhism, found at Mount Hiei, near Kyoto, Japan. They run (and quite often walk) for spiritual enlightenment. Their ultimate achievement is the completion of the 1,000-day challenge (over the course of seven years), which only 46 men have completed since 1885. Of these, three have completed the circuit twice, most recently Yusai Sakai, who first went from 1973 to 1980, then, after a half-year pause, finished his second round in 1987 at the age of 60.

Initially monks must cover 25 miles (40km) per day for 100 consecutive days. In the fourth and fifth years their target is 25 miles (40km) each day for 200 consecutive days. In the sixth year they must complete 37 miles (60km) each day for 100 consecutive days, and in the seventh year they have to do 52 miles (84km) each day for 100 consecutive days.

Along the way, monks need to stop at some of the 250 shrines and temples, and all runs are conducted in straw sandals, carrying books with mantras to chant. They also carry a knife and a rope, to be used by the monk if he fails, whereby he must take his own life, by hanging or self-disembowelment. Though this now appears to be a custom more honoured in the breach than the observance.

74

Derek Clayton is born
(17 November 1942)

Born in England and raised in Northern Ireland, Australian long-distance runner Derek Clayton is one of the greatest marathoners to never win an Olympic medal. The 6 foot 2 inch (1.88m) runner set a world best in the Fukuoka Marathon, Japan, in 1967 of 2:09:36.4 – the first sub-2:10 marathon.

He went on to break this time in Antwerp in 1969, with the first sub-2:09 marathon (2:08:33), which stood as the world best for nearly 12 years. The IAAF back his time. The ARRS, however, consider the course to have been short.

Clayton represented Australia at the 1968 Olympics in Mexico City, finishing in seventh place (2:27:23). Four years later he placed thirteenth (2:19:49) in the same event. He was said to run 160 miles (257km) per week.

75

The Galloping Granny is born
(24 November 1924)

As a child Mavis Hutchison suffered three nervous breakdowns and spent months in bed, all of which kept her away from sport. But the South African certainly made up for it. She had a spell as a race walker, then ran marathons and ultramarathons, rising to prominence in 1978 when the 53-year-old grandmother became the first woman to run across the US. The 2,871-mile (4,620km) route from Los Angeles to New York took her 69 days, two hours and 40 minutes.

Mavis has also run 1,000 miles (1,600km) from Pretoria to Cape Town in 22 days, twice, and a circuitous 2,000-mile (3,200km) run around much of South Africa in 1985. She set a new women's record for John O'Groats to Land's End in the UK and has set women's world records for 100-mile and 24-hour running.

She claims to be the third woman to ever finish the Comrades Marathon, in 1966, and has completed the race six more times.

Hutchison has also set South African W80+ masters records for 100m, 200m, 400m and 800m.

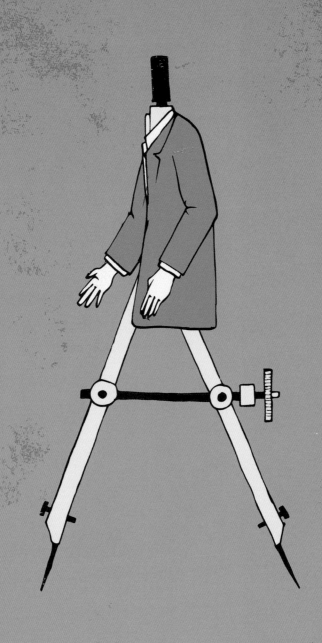

76

The original globe-trotter passes away
(4 December 1979)

In 1908, the Touring Club de France announced a contest for walking around the world, with a prize of 100,000 francs – a fortune then. The concept caught the imagination of four Romanian students studying in Paris. They learned languages, studied cartography, practised Romanian folk songs and dances (to perform in exchange for money en route), did weight training and walked 28 miles (45km) per day in preparation. In 1910 the group set out on their voyage accompanied by a dog, Harap.

In July 1911, in India, one of the quartet died of opium poisoning. Two years into the trip, another died, trying to cross a narrow mountain pass in China's Nanling Mountains. A third Romanian wanderer, suffering leg problems from an old accident, was advised to stop by doctors in Florida. So he (and the dog) did. After having both legs amputated, he died in 1915.

The final one of the gang of four, Dumitru Dan, put his trip on hold during World War I. But he completed it in 1923. Dan had crossed five continents, three oceans, been through 76 countries and worn out 497 pairs of shoes.

Guttingly for Dan, given post-war inflation however, the value of the prize (in current terms) had shrunk from about €500,000 to €40,000.

He had, however, earned a place in the *Guinness Book of Records* for being the first person to travel around the world on foot. He died on this date in his native Romania.

77

Rob de Castella sets world record at Fukuoka
(6 December 1981)

With a sustained drive over the final 7 miles (12km), Australia's magnificently moustached Rob de Castella won today's Fukuoka Marathon in a time of 2:08:18.

It was the fastest time recorded for an out-and-back course, but it wasn't initially known to be a world-best time. De Castella's 2:08:28 was five seconds slower than Alberto Salazar's at the same year's New York City Marathon.

But it later emerged that the New York course was about 162 yards (148m) short so de Castella's time was ratified as the world record.

Nicknamed 'Deek' or 'Deeks' in Australia, and 'Tree' by his competitors due to his thick legs and inner calm, Rob went on to win the Boston Marathon, the Commonwealth Games (twice) and, in 1983, the marathon World Championships.

In 2003 he launched a specialist chain of grain- and gluten-free bakeries and cafés, called Deeks.

78

Freak races
(11 December 1763)

In the UK in the seventeenth and eighteenth centuries, plain old running was clearly deemed a tad dull and a craze for 'freak races' gathered momentum. The more bizarre the concept, the more popular the spectacle. Sometimes both runners were equally comical, sometimes the freak was the superior and therefore handicapped runner. For example, in 1763 a race between a runner over 100 yards (91m) and a stilt walker over 120 yards (110m) was won by the latter. In the same year, a fishmonger tried to run from Hyde Park Corner, London, to Brentford with 56lb (25.4kg) of fish on his head. He bet he could do so in one hour, and did so with 15 minutes to spare. In another recorded instance, an unusually rotund gentleman raced against a young runner with a jockey on his back. Running was never this good again.

79

Kilian Jornet runs up Americas' biggest mountain
(23 December 2014)

Professional mountain athlete Kilian Jornet set a new speed record on Argentina's 22,841ft (6,962m) Mount Aconcagua, the highest mountain in both the southern and western hemispheres.

Jornet ran up and down the Normal Route, which ascends 13,327 vertical feet (4,062m) in around 50 miles (80km) round-trip to the summit and back. Starting at 6 a.m., the Catalan sped 15 miles (24km) to the Plaza de Mules base camp at 14,108 feet (4,300m), normally a two-day hike, then started the much steeper ascent of the mountain, reaching the summit about nine hours after starting – slower than he'd hoped. He made up time on the descent, covering just under marathon distance in less than four hours. He returned in 12:49. The previous record was thought to be 13:46.

Jornet has set speed records for Denali (previously Mount McKinley, Alaska, US), Mount Kilimanjaro (Tanzania), Mont Blanc and the Matterhorn (both Alps).

80

The Ancient Egyptian ultramarathoners
(29 December 1303–1213 BC)

It's impossible to put a date to it, but Rameses II (1303–1213 BC), pharaoh of Ancient Egypt, was a runner. He had to run, alone and in front of crowds, before his coronation to ostensibly prove himself worthy of the throne. Then he had to repeat the feat 30 years later at a festival, to clarify that he was still 'fit' for the job, and run the same one-man race every third or fourth year to prove he was still up to the task – right up until the age of 90. A physically weak king was seen as undesirable and the ceremony was thought to renew his powers.

The earliest known foot races, known as 'city races', can also be traced to Ancient Egypt, dating to 2035 BC, and (naturally) concluding with animal sacrifices.

In fact, Egyptian soldiers may have also run the first ultramarathons. Records point to a 62-mile (100km) race from Memphis to Fayum and back, run partially at night to avoid heat, in around 690–665 BC.

King Taharqa took part (for a bit anyway), and the winner of the 31-mile (50km) return leg took a very respectable four hours.

GLOSSARY

24-Hour Races

Typically taking place on a standard athletics track or 1- or 2-mile (1.6 or 3.2km) looped course, runners simply have 24 hours to see how far they can run.

Association of Road Running Statistics (ARRS)

An association independent of the IAAF which holds elite distance running records for distances of 3,000m and upwards.

Back straight and home or final straight

A standard 400m athletics track has two 100m straights and two 100m bends. The final 100m in a race is known as the home or final straight, while the other straight 100m is the back straight.

Commonwealth Games

Previously known as the British Empire Games, British Empire and Commonwealth Games, and British Commonwealth Games, an athletics championship event between athletes from Commonwealth nations, the 53 former British territories.

European Championships

A biennial (every two years) athletics championship event organised by the European Athletics Association since 1934. It used to be every year, but has been held every two years since 2010.

Fastest Known Time (FKT)

The assumed record for covering a certain route, which could be from a certain start point to the summit of a mountain, an established trail (such as America's Appalachian Trail) or a bespoke route.

Fells

Northern English word for mountains, from the old Norse word 'fjall'.

Final or home straight, see **Back straight**.

International Association of Athletics Federations (IAAF)
The world athletics governing body.

Interval Training or Intervals
Popular training method whereby an athlete runs at a fast pace for a
short time, then has a rest 'interval' (usually slower running), before
resuming the set of faster repetitions.

Kick
An increase of speed towards the end of a race.

Lactic acid
Anaerobic (high-intensity) exercise produces lactic acid in muscles
which makes them feel heavy and fatigued.

Oxygen deficit
When the lungs demand more oxygen than the runner is able to
breathe in. Not a situation that can be sustained for long.

PB
A runner's Personal Best time (known as Personal Record in the US).

Pedestrianism
The popular late-eighteenth and nineteenth-century sport of travelling
long distances, either around a track (six-day races attracted big crowds
for a several years) or DIY challenges such as Paris to Moscow in a
stipulated time, competitively and often for large wagers. Pedestrianism
was initially a walking challenge but transformed into a hybrid sport as
some pedestrians preferred to run, trot or shuffle. The practice can be
seen as the origin for both racewalking and ultramarathon running.

Six-day races Popular in the 1870s, attracting tens of thousands of spectators, this form of pedestrianism saw individuals race around a track usually in an arena for six days, with rest and sleep breaks. Though there are still some six-day races today, the 1870s Astley Belt series was the sport's apex, with Irish-American Daniel O'Leary and Charles Rowell the two biggest stars.

Ultramarathons Any running event longer than the modern marathon distance of 26.2 miles (42.2km).

World Championships The World Championships in Athletics is organised by the IAAF every two years. From 1983 to 1991 it was held every four years.

World Marathon Majors: The Tokyo, Boston, London, Berlin, Chicago and New York City Marathons. It works as both a championship event for elite runners (also including the World Championships and Olympic Games Marathons) and a challenge for amateur runners.

ACKNOWLEDGEMENTS

Though there were long hours, late nights and very occasional disagreements (always both minor and entirely amicable), working on this book has been hugely enjoyable – which isn't always how it goes.

That's down to both the fascinating subject matter, and also the very professional, personable and deadline-dodging forgiveness of the fine staff at Aurum Press. Especially Daniel Seex for his wonderful illustrations, the heroically diligent Ian Allen, Lucy Warburton, Daniela Rogers, Robin Harvie and everyone else involved.

A huge thanks also to Barbara and Kelvin for teaching me love the outdoors, as well as Jonathan Manning, Graham Coster, John Shepherd, Paul Simpson, Alyssa White, Paul Hansford, Mario Cacciottolo, Amy, Indy and Leif.

BIBLIOGRAPHY

This book required reams of research and some of the excellent books I used more extensively are:

Algeo, Matthew, *Pedestrianism: When Watching People Walk was America's Favourite Sport*, Chicago Review Press, 2014

Askwith, Richard, *Feet in the Clouds: A Tale of Fell-Running and Obsession*, Aurum Press, 2004

Finn, Adharanand, *Running with the Kenyans: Discovering the Secrets of the Fastest People on Earth*, Faber & Faber, 2013

Finn, Adharanand, *The Way of the Runner: A journey into the Fabled World of Japanese Running*, Faber & Faber, 2015

Harvie, Robin, *Why We Run: A Story of Obsession*, John Murray, 2011

Hawker, Lizzy, *Runner: A Short Story About a Long Run*, Aurum Press, 2015

Jean, Shirley & Tucker, Roll, *The Amazing Foot Race of 1921*, Heritage, 2011

Jornet, Kilian, *Run or Die: The Inspirational Memoir of the World's Greatest Ultra-Runner*, Viking, 2014

Jurek, Scott, *Eat and Run: My Unlikely Journey to Ultramarathon Greatness*, Bloomsbury, 2013

Karnazes, Dean, *Ultramarathon Man: Confessions of an All-Night Runner*, Jeremy P. Tarcher, 2006

Marshall, P S, *King of the Peds*, Author House, 2008

McDougall, Christopher *Born to Run: The Hidden Tribe, the Ultra-Runners, and the Greatest Race the World Has Never Seen*, Random House, 2010

Noakes, Tim, Pro, *Lore of Running*, Human Kinetics Europe, 2002

Owen, Paul, *The Joy of Running*, Summersdale, 2013

Sears, Edward S, *Running Through the Ages*, McFarland, 2001

Stevens, John, *The Marathon Monks of Mount Hiei*, Echo Point Books & Media, 2008

Sillitoe, Alan, *The Loneliness of the Long Distance Runner*, HarperCollins, 1959

Whitaker, Mark, *Running for Their Lives: The Extraordinary Story of Britain's Greatest Ever Distance Runners*, Yellow Jersey press, 2012

The excellent website www.racingpast.ca was also very useful.